THE **GOLDEN FOOTBALL**

**REPLACING ACCOUNT SERVICE
WITH ACCOUNT LEADERSHIP**

— MARK SCHOFIELD

Published by Lulu. www.lulu.com

Schofield, Mark.
The Golden Football. Replacing Account Service with Account Leadership.
Mark Schofield.—1st ed.

ISBN-13: 978-1-4303-1831-6
ISBN-10: 1-4303-1831-6

···

Design by Dave Alsobrooks (www.davealsobrooks.com)
Fonts: Tyrvania Regular, Italic, Small Capitals; Brothers Bold

10 9 8 7 6 5 4 3 2 1

First Edition

Dedication

To my wife Debbie, whose love
and support makes my life wonderful.

To my daughter Diana, whose spirit,
intellect, and heart inspires me.

To my mentor and friend Lloyd Jacobs, who shared
his wisdom, his instincts, and his humor
to make every day a mostly successful adventure.

To my mentor and professor Don Cushman,
who taught me how to think and then instilled
in me a sense of how much I could accomplish.

To my friend and colleague Emily Bright, whose skill
and insight made this book better.

THE GOLDEN FOOTBALL

TABLE OF CONTENTS

OVERVIEW

INTRODUCTION:
LET'S STOP EATING OUR YOUNG

Account service is dead. Account leadership is the future. Without leadership, there will be no future.

Over the last several years, I have made two polar opposite observations about account people working in the business. First, the account people I encounter are much better armed for our business in almost all ways than their predecessors. They are smarter, more curious, much more traveled, better educated, and did I say smarter? It really is amazing. They are articulate and interesting to talk to. They possess a basic self-assuredness that their lives are going to work out just fine. Oh, and I believe that this generation is very willing to work hard, under two conditions. Those conditions are they must feel a tangible commitment to help them succeed in their careers, and they want their agency to care about them on a personal level.

However, my second observation is that account people mostly don't know what to do. Or they lack understanding about how it should be done. The reason? Nobody told them. When you look at account groups in the same agency, there is such wide disparity in their approach, even in the reports they use. The quality of briefs varies tremendously between and within account groups. And, sadly, most briefs are just not very good.

estimates

Account people do not carry that same self-assuredness in their work as they do in their private lives. The nuances of listening to how a client says something, and what he does not say, how to handle objections, taking charge of situations, etc., and the myriad of subtle skills that a good account person must possess are too often missing. My mentor, Lloyd Jacobs would call today's account people "book smart, not street smart." I would call them doers, not leaders.

So, we have these budding stars who are not performing, for the most part, at a level of high contribution that agencies need today. They want to, but in many cases no one has showed them how.

As a result, we see among our account people massive frustration, low morale, and burn-out after only a few years in this business. In other words, we are eating our young.

Why is this happening and what difference can it make if the situation were improved?

FIRST, AGENCIES DO NOT SPEND TIME TO TRAIN THEIR PEOPLE. This applies even to the most rudimentary aspects of their job. It pains me to watch an account person struggle trying to figure out how to load job changes into the computer, get frustrated, try again, waste more time, then abandon the technology that was built to help them improve their productivity because no one taught them how to properly use the technology.

workamajig

Many account people have never learned how to make effective presentations. They understand the words on the creative brief form, but they don't know how to get into the heads of the target and really understand what might turn them on.

Now here is the really weird part. Virtually all agency chiefs know this. They understand the value of effective and capable account people. They also know that their account management department is often among the weakest in the agency. Yet little if any formal or even mentoring training takes place today.

SECOND, AGENCIES HAVE DILUTED THE RESPONSIBILITIES OF ACCOUNT PEOPLE.

Instead of training and developing account people, agencies have opted to give much of the client responsibility to creative, media, and planning people. It is stretching the point only a little bit to say most account people spend their time coordinating projects, scheduling meetings, and providing basic client service.

Strategy

THIRD, WEAKENING THE ACCOUNT FUNCTION HAS WEAKENED THE AGENCY.

Of course, some agencies have done a marvelous job of developing their account people, and many agencies have performed very well over the last few years. However, when we look across the landscape of the agency business, and the agency-client relationship, it cannot be denied that a serious deterioration has taken place.

Coincident with the weakening of the account function within the agency are these trends:

- Decrease in the average tenure of agencies and clients
- Decrease in the perceived value clients receive from agencies
- Decrease in compensation levels and margins that agencies enjoy
- Decrease in the sense of business partnership by the client toward the agency

That last point is especially worrisome. If account people are not capable of acting as a true business partner to their client, agencies are in trouble. Creative people and account planners want no part of that business relationship. Besides, due to their lack of business training most are not qualified to handle it.

FOURTH, CLIENTS NEED A BUSINESS PARTNER AND WELL-TRAINED ACCOUNT LEADERS MORE TODAY THAN EVER BEFORE.

Look at the situation at most client companies compared to years ago. Their staffs have been downsized but the workloads keep growing. Today, many clients come from disciplines other than Marketing. Some of my most recent clients were lawyers, plant managers, financial managers, and sales people. Many clients do not know how to manage a marketing function to accomplish company objectives. They can express an opinion like anybody else, but the savvy, insightful client who knows how to manage and nurture an agency to its greatest advantage is getting more rare every day. Like the agency side of the business, clients over-title their under-trained employees and place huge demands on them. So, clients need all kinds of counsel that goes well beyond the service of just making ads. They need leadership from their agency partners.

FIFTH, ACCOUNT PEOPLE, THEREFORE, MUST TAKE A MUCH MORE ACTIVE PERSONAL ROLE IN BECOMING A LEADER, NOT JUST A PROVIDER OF SERVICE.

This book is intended to provide that missing instruction. This book represents a call to arms to all people that work in creative services firms. The old account service function must be replaced by a whole new mind-set called account leadership. Account leadership provides direction and initiative for colleagues inside the agency. Account leadership provides proactive marketing counsel, business-building ideas and candor in a partnership with clients.

This book was written for account people by an account person. It represents a compilation of successful experiences, wisdom passed down to me from mentors, and plenty of lessons learned the hard way. These practical approaches have worked with large and small accounts, in large and in small agencies.

In my consulting practice, I position my service as "Accelerating the Future" for my clients. I hope this book will accelerate the future for account leaders at all levels of experience.

I would like to encourage other members of the agency who do not work in account leadership to take a peek at the book as well:

CREATIVE people can recognize the intended coaching points and encourage their account colleagues when they see attempts to live the leadership style and shed the service-only approach. There are a lot of benefits for the creative teams from the successful adoption by account people of the principles and lessons — awards, bigger budgets, more advocacy, to name a few.

MEDIA people can also benefit directly when the account leaders start to give them input that really helps craft even more creative media plans.

PRODUCTION people might want to encourage their account leaders to take a stronger stand with clients and within the agency so some of the great production ideas they think up can actually get implemented.

FINANCE people should be delighted when account people create incremental revenue, reduce costs by reducing do-overs, thereby increasing margins.

One last note. I recently took a poll among senior executives in 150 agencies. The question was: "List three skills that you would most like to see improved in your account group." The top vote getters were: presentation skills and listening skills. Receiving very few votes was leadership. Has senior management written off leadership as a fundamental expectation of the account management function? I hope not. This book intends to create the skill sets necessary to help our account people become invaluable leaders for their clients and their agencies.

We must stop eating our young. Let's nurture that inherent talent to the benefit of all.

How To Use This Book To Accelerate Your Future

"Let the book create questions that you want your boss to answer."

As long as you need to work for money, you might as well try to accomplish the most so you get the biggest raises, the largest bonuses, and the fastest promotions.

This book will provide a great return in lessons learned if the reader reads through the whole book the first time to get a good feel for the kinds of lessons that are contained herein. Several points may jump out at you right away that you want to begin to adopt. Don't try to memorize the book.

The book was written in "pods" or tightly focused subjects so you can use the book as a handy reference guide. You may come across an issue or problem that will bring to mind some point in the book that you can re-read to refresh your memory, or to give you a kick-start for your own thinking.

Let the book create questions that you want your

boss to answer. Write them down as you read, then schedule time with your supervisor. You two may come up with something terrific that is better than what is written in this book.

There is a small amount of overlap, even duplication, between some sections. This book should be read as an integrated, connective approach to successful account leadership.

One last thought. Read this book "aggressively." By that I mean when you read something that makes sense to you, think about how to put it into action in your work. If you read something that does not make sense to you, ignore it, and never think about it again.

Too many books get read, and then get put on the shelf, and the lessons never become actions. This book was written deliberately to stimulate actions that succeed.

When you adopt the suggestions contained in this book, and those suggestions work successfully for you, please do me a favor. Pass the suggestions on to someone else. Then pass on some successful experiences that did not appear in this book.

CHANGE THE NAME, CHANGE THE EXPECTATION

"So, WHY DON'T YOU START BY CHANGING THE NAME OF YOUR FUNCTION TO THE ONE THAT REALLY BEST DESCRIBES WHAT YOU WANT TO ACCOMPLISH?"

Three people walk into your office. They tell you their functions are, respectively, Account Service, Account Management, and Account Leadership.

Based solely on this information, how would you answer these questions:

- Which one is the most senior in experience?

- Which one will your client respect the most?

- Which one bills the highest rate?

- Which one would you rather ask to be your mentor?

- Which one would you expect to be the most capable?

If you answered "Account Leader," then your impression conforms to many other people with whom I have spoken. This book seeks to show you how to change the expectations of account people among all your colleagues and clients, and to show you how to exceed those elevated expectations.

So, why don't you start by changing the name of your function to the one that really best describes what you want to accomplish? In two agencies, I changed the name of the function to Account Leadership. Over time, many of those former account service people became leaders. Oh, and they succeeded by adopting the lessons espoused in this book.

THE GOLDEN FOOTBALL

My mentor, Lloyd Jacobs, taught me three key lessons about surviving as an account person in the agency business.

First, always work on more than one account. That way, if you lose one, you still have a job.

"ALWAYS WORK ON MORE THAN ONE ACCOUNT."

Second, always participate in New Business. Since New Business is the lifeblood of any agency, senior managers will appreciate — and reward — you for your contributions. Plus, if you help win a new client, odds are better that you will work on the account.

Communication
practice
pitches

"ALWAYS PARTICIPATE IN NEW BUSINESS."

And third, always keep the Golden Football in the client's end of the field.

"KEEP THE GOLDEN FOOTBALL IN THE CLIENT'S END OF THE FIELD."

The Golden Football represents the business-building initiative that you constantly put in front of your clients. They are ideas that the client did not ask for, and they didn't know they needed them. When you keep the client reacting to your initiatives (their end of the field), you maintain more power and value in the relationship. In turn, if you let the client throw ideas or problems at you, the agency is reacting rather than leading. And that is the quickest way to lose power and control of an account. An early danger sign in a relationship occurs when account people are sitting in their offices waiting for the phone to ring.

A recent study done by noted marketing consultant Tony Louw confirms the power of the Golden Football. He found that on average, account people believe that the agency should bring clients three to four new ideas per year. Clients, on the other hand, believe that agencies should bring them three to four new ideas each quarter. Huge difference.

This creates an enormous opportunity for you as an account person. Gather your team — creative, account, media, production, traffic and research — every month to brainstorm business-building ideas. Take those ideas to your client every month. Every Golden Football you present builds a bond of trust. It represents an example of the agency working hard to improve the client's business. The Golden Football represents leadership in action.

This probably sounds like a logical idea. And many of you may be saying, "We do that already." But I ask you — really? You meet as a team every single month and present ideas to your client, 12 times a year? If so, congratulations. Your group is a rare one. So rare, in fact, that you should mention this practice in your next new business pitch. Be prepared to show the prospect a list of ideas by month. I guarantee you no one will tell you, "My agency does that all the time." After all, any client working with an agency that presents Golden Football ideas every month isn't conducting a review.

~NoteS~

~NoteS~

Strategic Thinking

ANALYZE A CLIENT'S BUSINESS — QUICKLY

Account leaders will never know as much about their client's business as the client.

Account leaders must know the key success drivers, and the key metrics that measure those drivers, in order to become a valued partner.

Key success drivers are those critical variables that determine how or whether the client makes money. Once you understand what are those variables and what measures are used to track those variables, then you can stay on top of how those key numbers are trending — going up, going down, or staying flat.

There is no single set of measures that can be used for all clients. For example, in the restaurant business, one of the key measures is same store sales growth. In the cruise industry, one key measure is average passenger revenue per day. In the tobacco business, share of market is a key measure.

You need to know the key measures for the brand in total, for each of the major products or lines of business, by geography, etc. Certainly you will want to know how those measures compare to year ago or versus the last three years in order

> "KEY SUCCESS DRIVERS ARE THOSE CRITICAL VARIABLES THAT DETERMINE HOW OR WHETHER THE CLIENT MAKES MONEY."

> "THERE IS NO SINGLE SET OF MEASURES THAT CAN BE USED FOR ALL CLIENTS."

STRATEGIC THINKING · 16

to understand the trend dynamic.

One of the key measures that many clients worry about, and therefore the agency worries about, is "the budget." One client lamented to me that they were 16% behind their sales budget. I asked him how that sales number compared to a year ago, he said, "Oh, we are 23% ahead of last year." When I asked him why the budget was so high, he told me, "The company wants to split off our division and take it public."

So, in this case, the business was doing well compared to last year (in part due to the agency's efforts), yet the client was under pressure because his business fell behind a company-dictated, artificial number. The account leader needs to apprise himself of this total situation in order to manage the morale of his internal partners and remain sensitive to the pressures felt by his client.

When I am preparing to meet with the senior client, I ask my account leaders to prep me with what we are currently working on for them, any big problems they are facing, and how the key measures of the business are trending. Good account leaders can pull that summary together very quickly because they know what is important.

"THE ACCOUNT LEADER NEEDS TO APPRISE HIMSELF OF THIS TOTAL SITUATION IN ORDER TO MANAGE THE MORALE OF HIS INTERNAL PART- NERS AND REMAIN SENSITIVE TO THE PRESSURES FELT BY HIS CLIENT."

BECOME A GREAT THINKER

"WHAT DISTINGUISHES A POOR THINKER FROM A GOOD THINKER AND A GOOD THINKER FROM A GREAT THINKER?"

During my years as a Brand Manager, I learned the hard way what distinguishes a poor thinker from a good thinker and a good thinker from a great thinker.

I was presenting the marketing plan for my brand in front of forty people. However, there was only one person in the room that really counted: The Vice President of Marketing. He was new to the company, he was tough, and he was smart. When I stood up first to present my plan at 9:00 a.m., I had a sneaking suspicion that I was about to be made an example of in front of the entire Marketing Department. After six hours of non-stop grilling by the Vice President, I knew that at least that instinct on my part had been accurate.

Here was his message. He mostly agreed with my plan. But based on my weak defense of it, he was not confident that I really understood my business and that I hadn't gotten lucky. He wanted me, and everyone in that room, to learn how to be a great thinker. Here was his definition:

POOR THINKER. Thinking tends to

be fairly random, characterized by opinions not based in either fact or a logical thought pattern that makes sense. A poor thinker can get lucky once in awhile, but over the long-term he will make bad decisions, big mistakes, and worse, he will not know how to correct those mistakes or adapt and make the right decisions.

GOOD THINKER. A good thinker can lay out a path or decision that makes sense. They can back up that decision with either factual support or logic that makes sense. The problem with a good thinker is that the decision arrived at may not be the best decision that could be made.

GREAT THINKER. The great thinker can see several potential right decisions or courses of action, all of which can be defended by facts or logic. The key to great thinking is the ability to not only identify optional solutions, but also to be able to walk around each direction and to understand the advantages and disadvantages of each course of action. Through this rigorous process, the great thinker unearths the best solution.

It took me a couple months to recover from the humiliation I suffered at this planning conference at the hands of this Vice President of Marketing and to really understand the message. Twenty years after this experience, I would say that this lesson about becoming a great thinker was one of the very most important that I have learned. It is one I have diligently applied in my professional work.

UNEARTHING INSIGHTS IS NOT JUST FOR PLANNERS

I think by this time, both account leaders and account planners have learned that there is more to discovering insights than just talking to the consumer.

Account leaders now know that the projective techniques planners use are just that — techniques. They are not magic. Planners do not hold the special formula for creating great briefs. The discipline of looking at the world through unconventional eyes is one that the account planners have expanded for all of us. So now we can all play.

I want to share a thinking process that has yielded many successful insights. At one agency, we branded the process the "Brand Momentum Analysis."

The key to this process is locating the direction and the velocity of change. For example, knowing the share of market for a competitor is fine, but its much more valuable to know if that share is going up, down, or remains flat.

The Brand Momentum Analysis contains three components. A quick example using the cruise industry will show you what I mean:

> "PLANNERS DO NOT HOLD THE SPECIAL FORMULA FOR CREATING GREAT BRIEFS."

MARKETPLACE AUDIT. Look for changes in:

- Total category. The cruise industry growth was leveling off.

- Key competitors. The large competitors were either acquiring small competitors or putting them out of business. The top four competitors were increasing their share of the total cruise market.

- New products. New ship builds would increase capacity by over 50% in the next 5 years. The biggest competitors were building a disproportionate share of the new tonnage.

- Key segments. The short cruise market was growing faster than any other segment. People were taking more and shorter vacations throughout the year.

- Distribution. Travel agents were not growing fast enough to handle the future growth in new berths. Direct bookings would have to be considered for the first time in the industry if the companies wanted to insure they could meet the demand.

So, the marketplace change dynamic was offering clues about the future that we needed to understand.

CONSUMER AUDIT. Until recently, this area was the sole purview of the account planner. We need to understand how the product fits into the consumer's life. The insight many times comes from that intersection.

For the first time in history, the growth of first-time cruising was slowing. This represented a dark cloud on the cruise horizon. With 14 new ships being built, at about $350 million per ship to build at the time, a slowdown in the growth rate of first-timers was scary.

Even worse, consumers told us that they understood the concept of cruising and they found other vacation options more attractive. Wow, the basic premise of warm water cruising had always been "tell people about the cruise experience, build ships to accommodate that experience, and they will come." No longer.

For many people, cruising meant "over-eating, nothing for men to do, stuck on a tin can..." Not a pretty picture. Not the picture of a once in a lifetime experience that had characterized cruising for so many years.

Consumers were changing their relationship with and perception of the product. We were listening...

BRAND AUDIT. This investigation looks at the difference, or "gap," between the brand perceptions of the target and the assets of the brand that are provided by the company. When a gap is identified, one either must change the perceptions of the target, or change the assets. That gap is often a rich source of clues and insights.

○ We discovered that consumers who had experienced the brand loved it and ranked it very highly on many key attributes. Experienced cruisers who had not tried the brand were interested in it. But the non-cruiser expressed little interest in trying the brand.

○ When we described a set of assets without identifying the brand or even the cruise category ("would you be interested in a vacation that allowed you to...") the non-cruisers said they would love that vacation.

THE INSIGHT/OPPORTUNITY. From the analysis summary above, and I drastically synthesized a ton of work that was completed, we concluded that the brand needed to re-position itself not as a premier cruise brand, but a world-class vacation unmatched by any other. More adventurous on-board experiences/assets needed to be added. Experiences off the ship needed to be highlighted and new more exciting ones needed to be created.

Advertising that supports that new positioning has now been running for almost ten years. In that time, the brand has almost doubled in size.

Every agency follows their own process for getting smart about their client's business. Account leaders can, and must, fully participate in a manner outlined above in order that the right, most powerful, insight for the brand be uncovered.

LIVE THE PRODUCT

There is so much data available today that we can access to understand the targets for our client's brands. There is an abundance of information about their products as well.

But data is not insight. And insight is oftentimes not the outcome of facts as much as it is the reading between the data lines. Insight represents an interpretation of facts and observations. When a client asks me "how do you know it's right?" I tell them I use the same experience, expertise, and sensitivity they use when they decide to create a new product, to change a marketing plan, or to promote a subordinate. Any decision that is future-based, which most decisions are, must be based on more than just a rehashing of the past.

> "INSIGHT REPRESENTS AN INTERPRETATION OF FACTS AND OBSERVATIONS."

Account leaders can acquire clues to insight, and even unearth insights, by immersing themselves in the client's target, their distribution and in their products.

To gain insight into our cruise line brand, two creatives and two account managers spent several days on a cruise. In addition to engaging in the activities on and off the ship, (hey, someone had to do it) we went into the bowels of the ship to find out how such a wonderful cruise experience was created, week after week, with crewmembers that came from dozens of different countries and cultures.

We stopped in the kitchen between meals where the crew was washing the floor. On the floor sat three buckets. I asked what the three buckets contained. One was cleaning detergent, one was disinfectant, and one was rinse water. I asked why they couldn't combine the three buckets into two buckets and save some time. The answer? "Because then the floors would not be clean." That was a huge clue about the commitment the brand made to giving their passengers the very best experience possible.

I wanted to understand how travel agents sold, or didn't sell, our client's brand versus the other cruise brands and versus the other vacation options. So I picked a market, got a list of travel agent addresses, and I did some mystery shopping. I would vary my story so I could see how I was handled if I went in as a single, or married with family. I wanted to discover how cruising was brought up if I didn't mention it, whether my client's brand was mentioned and pitched before I mentioned it, and then how they steered me to a decision. Very enlightening.

Plant tours can tell you so much about both the product and the brand. The insight for the initial creative work for an automobile account came from a conversation the Account Director held with one of the automobile research engineers. After explaining about the past and current design innovations the company had created, the engineer told the account guy, "You must tell people what we do here." The Creative Director heard that comment and he created a campaign that spoke to the "soul of the brand."

We were beating our heads against the wall on a low-priced fast food chain. None of us had eaten at the franchise, and almost nobody in the agency wanted to do it. The target operated within a totally different socio-economic strata than most of us in the agency. We had done the focus groups, etc. Yet we still did not "get it." We were not connecting with the target on an emotional level. Then we decided to go spend a whole day in one of the restaurants. Two reluctant creatives and a couple of account people made the trip. The day was spent eating the food, watching and talking to the customers, and working in the back of the restaurant. We absorbed the essence of the target as they related to this dining experience.

It worked. We broke the emotional logjam. We finally "felt" the target. Learn. Absorb. Get behind the scenes. Ask the guy on the line about the products. Know more about your client's products, their distribution, and the connection between the product and the consumer's life than anyone in the agency.

THE KEY TO GREAT CREATIVE BRIEFS

All agencies possess some kind of form to fill out to produce a creative brief. I won't argue for the perfect form since I don't think one exists.

I want to point out the two most critical sections in the brief that will decide whether great work will be produced. The account leader can directly contribute to these two critical sections.

Who are we talking to? I still see "women 25-54" in creative briefs! First of all, the 54 year old could be the mother of the 25 year old. Their interests, their life stage, and their connection to even the same product or service (say, cruises or automobiles) are probably radically different. The creative team cannot concept great ideas for such an inconclusive/diffuse target.

"TELL THE CREATIVE TEAM ABOUT A PERSON. WRITE A STORY ABOUT HER. BRING HER TO LIFE."

Tell the creative team about a person. Write a story about him or her. Bring her to life. If she is 32, is she married, does she work, job or career, children, what is her life like in general, and specifically, how does she relate with the product or service? Does it provide a convenience, an indulgence, an emotional feeling, an escape, a practical solution, etc? Since a picture can say a thousand words, create a pictorial montage that brings her to life. Or, ask your production manager to create a video that shows snippets of her life.

Anything you can do to personalize and humanize the target for the creative team will be invaluable. The creative team can concept great ideas for someone they know.

What is the central idea? For iPod, the central idea was "Celebrate music." The idea opens up many directions to execute this idea. At the same time, "Celebrate music" is grounded in a fundamental truth about iPod. It is also a big, category-owning idea. It doesn't provide a lot of room for the next guy into the category.

Many powerful ideas come from simple truths about how people include products and services in their lives. The account group on Volvo Trucks talked to truckers at truck stops while they filled up their tanks, ate meals, and shot the breeze with fellow truckers. What they learned led them to understand that independent truckers have a "love affair" with their trucks. They think of their trucks as a home away from home, as an economic partner, as a safe haven from harm, as a trusted friend. Boy, did that insight open the way for the creative team to produce some powerful work.

Focus on "who" and the "central idea" and your creative partners may let you go to lunch with them once in awhile.

MEDIA PLANNING PRINCIPLES AND A CREATIVE MEDIA PLANNING PROCESS

"LIKE EVERYTHING ELSE IN OUR BUSINESS, MEDIA IS NOT ROCKET SCIENCE."

Wow, that sounds like a mouthful. Not really.

I want to help the account leader break down some of the psychological barriers many account people feel toward this discipline. Like everything else in our business, media is not rocket science. The best media thinkers I have worked with use smart strategic principles plus a creative twist to create a great plan.

SMART MEDIA PLANNING PRINCIPLES

OVERVIEW
(Sometimes clients forget these points)

○ A plan cannot do everything/ reach everyone — you must make choices/priorities

○ When you put emphasis on someone or something, you necessarily de-emphasize someone or something else.

STRATEGIC PRINCIPLES

1. Spending level — Understand what a media budget means in a competitive marketplace

    ○ Share of Voice (SOV)/ Share of Market (SOM).

- Maintain market position: SOV/SOM=100

- Invest to grow market position: SOV/SOM>100

- Milk the business, declining market position: SOV/SOM<100
    - Note: If SOV and SOM data is not available, % of budget/ % of sales is an acceptable approximation

- Meet/Beat Competition. Sometimes, you decide to spend what it takes to meet or exceed a competitor's SOV. A new product launch against a large competitor is one situation where this principle could be used.
    - Coaching tip: The 20% factor. All media plans should include an incremental 20% in spending for tactics that would go above and beyond the recommended plan. The rationale is "this is how we would recommend you spend the next X amount of money if it were available." Prioritize the 20% by most critical tactic first, then the next, etc. so the client could approve a portion of the incremental 20% rather than all or nothing.

    The potential revenue-increasing benefits to the agency are obvious.

2. Geography — how to allocate your money against geography

- Fish where the fish are (% of budget= % of sales)

- Invest to build a territory (% of budget> % of sales)

- Milk a territory (% of budget< % of sales)

3. Media choices

- Do a complete job in one medium before moving to the next medium. This means media priorities must be assigned

  - For example, 100 GRPs per week for each flight in TV, #50 showing in out of home, etc.

  - Define what a flight must be (e.g. 4 weeks in TV)

- Use multiple media. Define each medium's role for the brand, given the brand's problems and opportunities

4. Seasonality

- Spend during the high season when sales are concentrated, or

- Spend during the "shoulders" of the high season to expand the high season, or

- Spend during the low season when competition is quiet, maximize SOV/SOM

5. Target Audience Definition

- Write a description of the consumer. Borrow the profile from the Creative Brief

- Fish where the fish are (get more fish like your current users)

- Fish where the category is, expand your brand's appeal

  - For example, your brand is old, category is younger, and so you spend against a younger target

6. Major Competition

◦ Decide who is your competition. They could be one or more of the following:

> ◦ Brand trying to appeal to the same benefit as yours (e.g. Audi and Volvo for safety)
>
> ◦ Brand who is vulnerable to my company (e.g. Cadillac is vulnerable to Audi)
>
> ◦ Brand who my brand is vulnerable to (e.g. Audi is vulnerable to BMW)
>
> ◦ What is their spend level and their SOV/SOM? What media do they use? What message?
>
> ◦ What is their three-year performance?

7. Different and Smarter

Unless you can outspend your competition, you must do something that they are not doing. So many brands follow the category leader media mix with less ammunition. How can they possibly expect to win?

8. Historical Perspective

Sometimes insights can be unearthed by looking at past plans and understand what worked and what did not work.

9. Sacred cows

Client preferences, legal sensitivities, etc. The sooner you get these on the table, the easier will be the workload for the media team.

If you can address these media principles for the planning team, they will love you because you have given them the grist from which to create great plans.

CREATIVE MEDIA PLANNING PROCESS

Traditional media plans are transforming quickly into "contact plans," "guerilla" or "viral" marketing. They all refer to intercepting the consumer where they live and those touch points get more complex all the time. Therefore, media plans have taken on a much more creative flair in terms of variety of message content delivery than ever before. So, should we not treat the planning process in a more creative way than in days past? The answer, of course, is yes! In fact, at two agencies, we duplicated for media the process that we used for creative. Here it is:

1. Review media brief internally.

2. Obtain client approval.

3. Conduct an internal mid-point review. Just like with creative, the media team brings ideas to the meeting. Some are fully cooked, some are initial concepts. But at this stage, there are no charts, no budgets, just ideas. The media team gets feedback from the account, and creative, team members. Then, the media team goes back to work.

4. Conduct a client mid-point review. The ideas may be fleshed out a bit more for this meeting. But still, no numbers, no Xs in boxes. Just ideas.

5. Conduct a finalized internal plan review.

6. Client presentation of finalized plan.

The first time we tried this new process, we were all a little nervous, especially with the client. Hey, clients aren't the only ones who resist change. But, the process worked quite well and the resulting plans were a huge creative leap forward compared to the past. If you want more creative media plans, take a clue from the process that generates creative ideas. Make sense?

~NoteS~

~Notes~

CLIENTS

THE "THREE-CLIENTS-IN-ONE RULE"

"LIFESTYLE DYNAMICS
AND CHOICES
INFLUENCE ALL
OF YOUR CLIENTS'
BEHAVIORS AND
OPINIONS."

Nearly all the account people I know possess extensive knowledge about their client —

the kind of humor they will approve in an ad, how tolerant they'll be to cost overages, their sensitivities regarding company politics, etc. And those things are good to know, but they are also just the price of admission.

In order to become an effective partner and a truly exceptional account leader, you must know your clients beyond the realm of their job responsibilities.

Every single client is really made up of three distinctive people:

1. A job title — Marketing Manager for instance. Like I said, any junior AE worth his salt already knows this person.

2. A corporate employee — your client's psychological place in the company. This encompasses their ambitions, fears, corporate friends and enemies, and how they perceive their own value within the corporation. For example, your client may be a "rebel," willing to take a few risks to help him stand out. Or he may really need the agency to be

his "voice," to float ideas up the line to his bosses. Either way, it's critical for you to understand your client's "corporate self."

3. A private citizen — the person who lives outside of the office. What do their spouses do for a living? What are their children's names? Are they saving for their kid's private school tuition or buying a second home at the lake? These lifestyle dynamics and choices influence all of your clients' behaviors and opinions.

As my mentor and long-time boss, Lloyd Jacobs, taught me, "If you know their hopes, dreams, fears, and their underwear size, it makes it that much harder to fire you."

As usual, Lloyd was clear, graphic, and insightful.

WHY AGENCIES LOSE ACCOUNTS

Agencies lose accounts every day, and often, they are caught completely off guard. But clients almost always send out danger signals long before the agency is fired.

And when they do, every account leader, from the most junior to the most senior, must tune into these early indicators of trouble and act quickly.

Contrary to popular myth, it is rare that inferior creative work is the reason for agencies to get fired. There are three predominant reasons that agencies lose accounts:

1. Management changes. New clients are not comfortable inheriting an agency. Ever. They fear the inherited agency may be better connected than they are to senior management. Therefore, the agency must move quickly to make themselves the new client's agency. The urgency for action is very high. Now, many of you may be thinking "everyone knows this." Really? If everyone knows this simple truism, why is it that almost every agency group I have witnessed do not make the new client priority number one, even above New Business? If we know it, but do not act on it, we have ignored the danger at our peril.

> "WHEN BUSINESS GOES BAD, CLIENTS GET NERVOUS BECAUSE THEY BECOME VULNERABLE WITH THEIR MANAGEMENT. FIRING AN AGENCY CAN BUY THEM TIME WHILE THEY 'FIX' THE PROBLEM."

A contact plan should be developed immediately that includes dates, assigns people, and topics. Those topics must include both social as well as business activities. Face time is never going to be more critical. Phone and e-mails are fine, but they do not substitute for "eyeball to eyeball." Remember, you want to become his/her agency. Fast. Bring ideas. Get those Golden Footballs teed up.

2. Financial reversals. When business goes bad, clients get nervous because they become vulnerable with their management. Firing an agency can buy them time while they "fix" the problem. Again, the agency needs to act quickly, get tactical and create short-term initiatives to show that the agency understands his/her anxiety. Action, action, action. Demonstrating partnership during the darkest times will make a disproportionately positive impression on the client.

3. Clients feel unloved. There are many ways that clients may describe this feeling:

"My business isn't getting enough attention."
"The agency never listens to me."
"Things are falling through the cracks."
"My people don't feel like they're being taken seriously."
"The agency isn't as responsive as they used to be."
"There aren't enough people servicing my account."

Many times, junior account people hear these rumblings before they are aired at a more senior level. I call it "scraping away at the base of the castle walls." The senior agency people are standing on top of the parapet with the senior clients, staring out over the client's kingdom. That scraping can start an erosion of the relationship until the agency partners receive the dreaded "we're going to look at our options" phone call.

Every client the agency touches gets the love. Face time, fresh ideas, and more of the same. When a client feels unloved, it is prudent to treat the account as a new business prospect with that sense of urgency.

SELF-ANALYSIS OF OUR CLIENT RELATIONSHIPS

There are many" bad news" messages that account leaders receive in performing their jobs:

"The ad budget was cut."

"The Creative Director hates the creative brief."

"Your most talented subordinate just resigned."

But the worst message an account leader receives is without question some version of "the client is taking the account elsewhere."

Believe me, that news is a kick in the stomach on so many levels. And it feels the same, at least initially, whether the client is large or small, or whether the client is the greatest or worst ever.

"BUT THE WORST MESSAGE AN ACCOUNT LEADER RECEIVES IS WITHOUT QUESTION SOME VERSION OF "THE CLIENT IS TAKING THE ACCOUNT ELSEWHERE."

In fact, losing one of your accounts is so painful that once it happens to you, your view of this business will be forever changed. So, you want to avoid suffering that experience as much as possible. Many of the topics I address in this book are intended to arm you to retain your clients.

One of the disciplines that helps keep us on our toes regarding "how we are doing" with our client relationships is to quarterly conduct a client relationship self-analysis. This is a team exercise and the word "team" means representatives of every function that touches the account.

How would our clients answer the following?

○ Have we kept our promises to this client?

○ Have we proactively brought business-building ideas to our client?

○ Do we have a professional relationship established with each of the key decision-makers?

○ Will they recommend us without reservation?

If the answer to any of the questions, especially the last one, is anything but "hell yes" then there is work to do, an action plan to create, and right now. One of the most consistent failings I see in agency account leaders is a lack of urgency in dealing with client relationship problems. The only reason I can think of to explain this phenomenon is the account leader has not yet gotten that dreaded phone call. And if you have received that phone call, and you still lack a sense of urgency in reacting to client relationship problems, you really ought to find another occupation.

How do we deal urgently with a "no" to any of the above questions?

Create an action plan that is specific in time, in action, and ownership "Until further notice, Alice will conduct all weekly status meetings in person at the client's office."

" John will create four sales promotion ideas by Friday, to be presented to the client by no later than next Wednesday, April 6."

The senior most account leader will personally supervise the execution of the game plan. No excuses from anyone on the team. No "I have to get a media brief done so Friday is out." Solving relationship problems becomes a very high priority just like new business. No one would think of saying, "I can't get my piece of the new business pitch done on time because I have other things to do." This has the same, if not more urgency as new business because current clients are paying you today.

Review the section on "Active and Proactive Paranoia" to keep the proper focus.

CLIENT ORIENTATION

"THE CLIENT MARKETING TEAM HAS JUST PUT THEIR BIGGEST RESPONSIBILITY, AND THEIR CAREERS, IN THE HANDS OF VIRTUAL STRANGERS."

What happens first when you win a new account (after the contract is signed and written expectations are agreed upon)?

Most agencies schedule some kind of visit to the client to meet the people, get a plant tour, review the state of the communication plans, compile an immediate To Do list, and collect all the market research that is available.

Ok, then what? Most agencies get right to work, making plans, making ads, trying to make a good impression as quickly as possible, right?

I would like to suggest that you consider taking a step before you start your work. Invite to the agency as many clients as you can get to attend, for a half-day client orientation.

Why? Let's think about it. The client marketing team has just put their biggest responsibility, and their careers, in the hands of virtual strangers. Doesn't it make sense to take some time at the very beginning of the relationship to get acquainted in a professional, and ideally in a social environment, so your new clients start off in a more comfortable frame of mind? Of all of the new accounts I have managed, I don't think I held a client orientation meeting in more than one third of the cases. Not smart. Looking back, it is obvious to me that many of the early bumps in the road the agency endured with the client could have been avoided, or handled in a much easier fashion, had we conducted that half-day orientation in the very beginning.

Most clients do not know how the agency does its work for them, or exactly what their role should be at any point in the process. We need to tell them!

Here is a suggested agenda for a client orientation meeting that worked quite well for us. Treat it as an example and modify it to suit your particular situation.

SUGGESTED PRE-MEETING AGENDA — DINNER

The client should visit your city the night before the meeting so you can enjoy dinner and get to know each other in a very social environment. Of the three meals, I have found that dinner is the best environment to bond with your client. The work day is over, dinner is usually an enjoyable, unhurried dining event, and the time pressure is less binding since there is nothing scheduled after dinner.

Things to remember:

- This is a business meeting, despite the social atmosphere you create.

- Place the clients next to the appropriate agency people. Clients never mind being asked to sit in a particular seat.

- Limit your alcohol intake. This goes for all business meetings.

- Be mindful what you say. Trust me, the client will remember the comment long after he or she forgets that everyone was just "having fun."

Meeting Set-Up

Let the client know before the meeting that the dress code will be business casual and the length of the meeting will take about 2 hours not including an agency tour or other subjects. Also, I suggest that the account team remain for the whole meeting. Other members of the team should come in to present their part of the agenda and then leave.

Everyone who touches the client's business should at least meet the clients. Perhaps you arrange a lunch in the agency and invite everyone who will touch the account. The atmosphere is social and the client will be impressed by the surprising number of people who work on their business.

Suggested Meeting Agenda

1. What kind of partner we (the agency) want to be. This provides an opportunity for your senior management to set the tone for how you want to partner with the client. Don't make this the Gettysburg address, but you will want to reinforce your brand positioning and apply your core values to the client's interests.

2. How would you (client) like the agency to communicate with you? Some people prefer the phone, some prefer e-mail. Cell phone numbers should be exchanged. There maybe some standing meetings that the client wants an agency representative to attend. All issues that relate to day to day communication should be discussed.

3. The production process.

◦ Make a big circular chart of each step of the process. Highlight those activities that require the client's involvement. I cannot tell you how many clients expressed surprise at all the steps that were required to make an ad.

○ Show physical examples of control documents. Tell the client they can be modified to suit the client.

  · Creative brief
  · Work order
  · Conference reports
  · Status reports
  · Estimates
  · Production schedules
  · Media and production spend to date

○ Tell the client that when there is a rush, the agency goes through all the steps, just faster. Let them know that rush jobs are always more expensive, and represent a greater chance for error.

4. Standard creative turn-around times. Of course you can turn ideas around in a day. You need to explain the benefits to the client of following these guidelines as often as possible. Solicit the client's input and agreement.

5. Production systems.

  · Weekly production meetings
  · Production log
  · Proofing
  · Hot lists
  · Revisions after approval cost money and affect the timeline

6. Media

○ How we work

  · Integral to strategic process
  · Integrated approach (media neutral)
  · Media Brief

- Planning process (include standard timelines for each step)
- Buying process
- Advantages to advanced media planning — the annual plan

○ What we need from the client

- Budget parameters
- Flexibility and freedom to develop innovative solutions
- Target audience data
- Geographic, seasonal buying data

7. How to be a Great Client

- Tell a bad client story
- A great client helps us do great work...
- Provide one focused direction. One client. One direction!
- Demand our best work. Then fight internally for that work
- Provide accessibility for approvals
- Line up internal people for approvals
- Let us present the creative work to you in person. Here is why...
- Let us help you present the work internally
- When things change, stay on our side of the table

8. Smooth financial function

- Explain the contract terms regarding estimates, payment timelines, late fees
- Engage the client in understanding who approves the bills
- Remind the client that the agency is not a bank
- Plan to get the agency's CFO to visit the client's CFO to get acquainted. Your CFO should also meet anyone below the CFO who handles invoices and estimates. When a problem occurs, people who know each other can resolve the issues much more easily than if they are strangers.

Of all the suggestions you will read in this book, this one pays the largest dividends in the early stages of the agency-client relationship for relatively little effort by the agency.

CONTROL DOCUMENTS

Two of the account leader's most important responsibilities are to manage the client's money and his projects.

MONEY

In my work with many agencies, I was surprised to learn that not everybody uses the following control documents to keep track of their client's money. Whew. If I could not account for every dollar of my client's money, I would have even more trouble sleeping. See if these documents make sense to help you become good fiscal stewards.

"IF YOU WANT TO SCARE YOURSELF, ADD UP THE CURRENT AMOUNT OF MONEY THE AGENCY HAS SPENT ON PROJECTS FOR YOUR CLIENT THAT DO NOT HAVE A SIGNED ESTIMATE."

1. ESTIMATES

This is an obvious one, yet so many projects are started without an estimate. Just know that the agency has no claim for any money if there is not an estimate signed by the client. If you want to scare yourself, add up the current amount of money the agency has spent on projects for your client that do not have a signed estimate. Then imagine that the agency does not collect half that amount. Then imagine how many people's bonuses, including your own, just went up in smoke.

2. PRODUCTION SPENDING BY PROJECT VERSUS ESTIMATES

Many agencies use software programs to collect this information. But many account leaders do not regularly monitor costs incurred as compared to the estimate while the job is in progress. Then they discover, to their horror, the costs have gone way overboard. Develop a routine, at least weekly, in which you review your costs incurred versus estimate.

3. MONTHLY PRODUCTION RECAPS

Prepare these reports for your client each month. Two benefits result. First, preparing the report forces you to get into the habit of reviewing your cost situation. Second, preparing this report for the client gives the client that comfortable feeling that their agency is keeping a close watch on their money. That builds trust, which helps when you ask them to approve the "edgy" creative work.

4. MONTHLY MEDIA SPENDING RECAPS

This report tracks the approved budget for the month and year-to-date, actual spending for the month and year-to-date, and the percent of the total year budget that has been committed to date.

If the account leader manages the above documents, he or she will create a positive and trusting relationship between the agency and the client. An excellent indicator that the agency has earned a level of trust with the client is when a client asks you, "can we afford to do such-and-such project?"

PROJECTS

The great thing about developing control documents for the client is that you are doing the same work for internal control purposes.

1. INTERNAL PRODUCTION SCHEDULES

Every phase of every project should be reviewed at least weekly with the creative, traffic, and production teams.

2. WEEKLY STATUS REPORTS

The terrific account leader takes the client through the status report, as opposed to just e-mailing it to them. That cements in the client's mind that the agency is working effectively. Also, it forces the client to review the report. Clients are extremely busy with activities that agency people don't see. If not forced to review all the projects, clients may ignore the report in order to handle their crisis of the moment. It is not wise to let your client drift very far from the day to day activities the agency is performing for them. "Selective memory" sometimes invades the client mind, and that makes for lots of headaches for the agency. Keep your client on task.

3. CONFERENCE REPORTS

This is the age-old CYA document that can save your life. It is also a document that is easy to avoid doing due to the crush of activity. Resist the temptation to avoid writing conference reports. There is no other document that chronicles the agreements between the agency and the client. With that document, you can defend the agency's actions, for example, spending money on the client's behalf if you have to move faster than the estimate process will allow. Without it, you are at the mercy of the client's "selective memory."

Complete them within 48 hours, at the latest. Memories fade, and the pace of activity can render them obsolete in a short time.

4. HOT LIST

When time is tight and you must have daily decisions from the client in order to make the deadlines, create a daily list of those decisions. List the decisions and number them. Ideally, you would coordinate with the client's assistant to receive the e-mail the night before and place the list in the client's chair so they see it first thing in the morning. Repeat this process every day until the crisis has past. Obviously, you don't want to make a practice of intruding on your client like this unless it's critical. But when it is... utilize the Hot List. This is another example of providing leadership for your client.

DRESS FOR THE CLIENT

"THE UNDERLYING ISSUE WAS CLEAR: THE SENIOR TEAM DID NOT FEEL CONFIDENT UNLESS THEY WERE DRESSING MORE FORMALLY THAN THEIR CLIENTS. WE NEEDED TO WORK ON THEIR SELF-CONFIDENCE AS WELL AS THEIR WARDROBES."

I admit I never really thought about this dictum (seems so obvious) until I joined an agency in which the dress code was always formal.

Mind you, I am talking about the new millennium here. Men wore suits and ties to all client meetings, and women wore whatever constituted suits and ties for them.

I asked the senior team one day, "Do your clients all dress so formally? Oh yes," they insisted. Ok. I thought this was a little weird in this day and time, but I was the new kid on the block, so I complied. Then I started attending client meetings, and clients began to visit the agency. Guess what? Most clients wore business casual clothing to their offices and they really dressed down for visits to the agency.

I started to needle the senior team about looking like a bunch of bankers instead of hip, cool ad folks. Well, I was told, we feel like we look more professional and we think we should dress up more than the client, to show respect for the client. And boy, they were not changing their mind.

So I started to wear business casual

attire to all meetings (except for two formal clients.) I also asked the clients what they thought about our agency dressing so formally. One client told me, "I really like the agency, but they do look awfully stiff compared to the rest of us when they come to our building."

I eventually wore most of the account people down (the creatives bought in immediately and may have gone a bit too far a few times) so they learned to dress for the client.

The underlying issue was clear: the senior team did not feel confident unless they were dressing more formally than their clients. We needed to work on their self-confidence as well as their wardrobes.

Mock turtlenecks are a whole lot more comfortable than ties!

FEEL THE AIR

Have you ever noticed that each company you visit seems to have a personality of its own?

IBM does not feel the same as Nike. They are two completely different companies in personality and in the vibe they give off.

One of the really valuable survival tools you want to acquire is the ability to "feel the air" when you visit a client's office. Once you get a feel for the normal vibe, you become sensitive to changes in the norm. For example, you may get off the elevator on the client's floor and you get a distinctly different feel than normal. It may feel uptight, or it may feel more upbeat that usual. You will want to determine its origin before your meeting starts. The answer could provide you with an early warning or it could signal a potential opportunity.

> "ONCE YOU GET A FEEL FOR THE NORMAL VIBE, YOU BECOME SENSITIVE TO CHANGES IN THE NORM."

I have found the quickest way to determine the validity and origin of the changed vibe is to ask the assistant to the most senior executive you know. One of the reasons those people are good at their jobs is that they have developed a very finely tuned sense of vibes in the office, especially as it relates to their boss. So I used to just ask that executive assistant, "Barbara, I am getting a feeling that folks are just a bit wound up today. What's up?" Barbara filled me in, and I felt that much more prepared for the meeting and the whole day.

If you can't get an answer from someone, trust your gut and stay extra alert. It may save your meeting.

"IF YOU CAN'T GET AN ANSWER FROM SOMEONE, TRUST YOUR GUT AND STAY EXTRA ALERT."

FOLD YOUR TENT

"HEED YOUR INSTINCTS. YOUR WORK WILL SHINE JUST AS BRIGHTLY NEXT WEEK."

Sometimes, hopefully not often, your antenna will tell you that the conditions are just not right to show ideas to the client.

When that happens just before a meeting in the client's building, it can be very awkward for everyone on your team. Any number of reasons could create the vibe: unexpected bad business results, an extraordinary calamity with a client employee, or a total pre-occupation with some other major activity like a buy-out, a merger, layoffs, a huge board meeting, etc. These clues might tell you that the ideas will not get a fair hearing by the client.

Do not present the work. Just be honest. "Look, with so much going on around here right now, this is not a good time to show you our ideas. Let's re-schedule."

Most clients will understand and go along with you. Every one of the above examples happened to me at some point, and not once did the client get offended, or force the agency to show the work.

Several clients actually admired the commitment to protect the work. The other members of my team, especially my creative partners, were very grateful in return.

Heed your instincts. Your work will shine just as brightly
next week.

EXCEPTIONS TO "NEVER SAY NO"

Account leadership does not inherently recognize the word "no."

George Patton didn't provide service, or management. He provided leadership. He provided "yes we can and yes you will." In an exaggerated way, he motivated his troops by not giving them an excuse for failure. He represented the quintessential "yes" man. In more than two decades in the agency business, I only remember ever saying "no" to our creative teams on a handful of occasions. In each case, the little voice inside my head was screaming "do not do it." Two examples:

"IN FACT, I FEARED THAT THE CLIENT WOULD EITHER BE OFFENDED OR QUESTION WHETHER WE REALLY UNDERSTOOD THEIR BRAND ESSENCE."

CASE #1

We created a design look for some cruise line posters. When I looked at the design, something told me that I had seen something like it before. When I asked the team, they assured me that no such design look existed. I don't consider myself an advertising historian by any means, but something was not right.

"THEY PUFFED OUT THEIR CHESTS AND DECLARED THAT THIS CAMPAIGN WAS GOING."

Upon checking several old seafaring books, I came upon the design that I vaguely remembered. It looked a lot like our work. Not exactly, but it was very close. So I told the creative team that we could not show the client this look. Well, to say I was not a popular teammate was a gross understatement. This was a powerhouse creative agency, a powerhouse team was working on the project, and the two design looks weren't identical. After a lot of gnashing and wailing, I told the team in a quiet voice, "Guys, this agency doesn't do work that looks anything like someone else. If the client sees our work as a knock-off of the older work, our credibility will get a big black eye. I am sorry, its beautiful work, but we are not going to present it." In the end, we presented some other designs that both the creative team and the client loved.

CASE #2
We worked for years at McKinney to get a shot at one of the large Ralston-Purina brands. Finally, the moment was right to develop work for the Wonder Bread brand (owned by Ralston.) This was a big opportunity for the agency, and we all worked our fannies off to prepare a great presentation. One of the campaigns we developed made fun of moms.

The alarm bell went off. While the twist made the campaign funny, it was at the expense of mothers who cared for their children by feeding them the bread that "builds strong bodies 12 ways." In fact, I feared that the client would either be offended or question whether we really understood their brand essence. I took my fear to the creative team and this time, they would not budge. They puffed out their chests and declared that this campaign was going "unless Chick (Charles McKinney) says no."

That usually made account people run for cover. I said ok, and I went to talk with Chick. I explained how I thought that this idea could undermine our whole effort to establish ourselves as a big-time player at Ralston. Chick grumbled and said he would think about it. Nothing more was said about the subject. I noticed that the bags of work we took to the client did not include that campaign.

Not only do we owe it to our client, but we owe it to our agency to do the right thing. When the alarm bell goes off... Don't hit the snooze button.

How To Be Actively And Proactively Paranoid

A CEO of a large packaged goods company once shared with me the old saw "Just because you are paranoid doesn't mean that someone isn't out to get you!"

One Monday morning, I breezed into the office of my boss, Lloyd Jacobs, to say good morning. Right away, I knew he had not enjoyed a great week-end. His face was red, and it was puffed up like a bulldog. I asked him what was the matter.

"It's too quiet. Too damn quiet." I asked him, "what are you talking about?" He stared at me with a glare. "How is the Royal Caribbean account going?" I told him things were smooth for the moment. We tended to have our ups and downs with this client, who was at the time our largest account.

"These issues, and the general "feel" of the client should be discussed among the account team on a regular basis, minimum weekly and before and after every client meeting."

Lloyd leaned over the desk and bellowed, "Exactly what I just told you. It's too quiet. Something is happening there, and we don't know about it. Let's gather the creative team and put our heads together."

Lloyd was the poster child for paranoid account people. He saw disaster looming around every corner. But Lloyd almost never got a nasty surprise by one of his accounts. He wanted us to constantly keep our ear to the ground and our eyes open for anything that might spell trouble for the agency. And then, trouble or not, he wanted us to take some action to head off the trouble or to prevent trouble from cropping up.

Remember the three primary ways agencies lose accounts?

° Management changes

° Financial reversals

° Client feeling unloved

These issues, and the general "feel" of the client should be discussed among the account team on a regular basis, minimum weekly and before and after every client meeting.

Lloyd and I used to use the following metaphor. I would tell him, "I see a dust cloud on the horizon. I don't yet know if it's a dust storm or the Indians are coming. Let's watch carefully. Even better, let's prepare in case it's the Indians." Lloyd always supported getting prepared ahead of time.

When you act, act urgently, not panicky. Develop a game plan fast. Get in front of the client ASAP. Above all, do not let the client feel your urgency. They should feel like you are all over their business, which will please them.

The very best way to act proactively paranoid is to keep the Golden Football constantly at the client's end of the field. Ideas, ideas, ideas. Make the client react to you.

PROFILE YOUR CLIENT AND YOUR CO-WORKERS

A very good discipline for getting to know your clients, and your co-workers, is to create a notebook (hard copy or electronic) that summarizes all pertinent facts about them.

There is magic in writing down important information. You learn it, then you have a record so you can easily access it to refresh your memory. Plus, you can pass it along to a colleague who comes onto the account so they can get quickly up to speed.

Create a template for this document. Include whatever logical set of information that makes sense to you. For example:

Name:

Title:

years at company

Prior company/work experience

Marital status (name, age of spouse/partner, his/her job)

Children: Names, ages, note special activities, health, interests

Personality description of the client/colleague

"THERE IS MAGIC IN WRITING DOWN IMPORTANT INFORMATION. YOU LEARN IT, THEN YOU HAVE A RECORD SO YOU CAN EASILY ACCESS IT TO REFRESH YOUR MEMORY."

Special likes/dislikes re their
professional work

Professional strengths

Personal interests, passions, health

Corporate ambitions, challenges

Review your profiles periodically and update them as necessary. This is a very easy way to force you to get to know your colleagues. Recall in another section "Three Clients in One," we discussed how a client leads a personal life, a corporate life, and a job life. The same applies to your agency colleagues as well.

TAKE A WALK IN THE CLIENT'S SHOES

"YOU WILL EITHER READ THAT FOUR INCH THICK PILE AFTER THE KIDS GO TO BED AND IGNORE YOUR SPOUSE, OR YOU WILL ARISE AT 4:00 AM SO YOU CAN READ IN PEACE AND QUIET."

Account leaders should be clients for a day.

Then you could come to work at 7:00 a.m., sit through several mind-numbing meetings, get second-guessed by marketing, senior management, sales, production, purchasing, and finance. Then you get to prepare status reports on what should have been accomplished last week, last month, last quarter, and last year. Next you meet with your boss to review what you are going to accomplish next week, next month, next quarter, and next year. In the afternoon, you return between 40-100 phone messages and/or e-mails.

Now, you are ready to meet with the agency that is all excited about presenting some creative ideas that promise to "really blow you away." You love the ideas. But, the cost to produce this mind-blowing work exceeds your already-raided-once-by-Finance marketing budget. You must give the agency this news after they present this world-beater campaign. After trying to comfort the agency with "we may get that money back in the fourth quarter," you pack up your reading in-box as you leave the office at 7:15 pm.

You will either read that four inch thick pile after the kids go to bed and ignore your spouse, or you will arise at 4:00 am so you can read in peace and quiet. Almost forgot, you then will check the additional 60 e-mails you received in the afternoon when you were meeting with the agency. Wow, give me a shot at being a client. Sweet!

The rather obvious point is that your client is very busy with activities that have little or nothing to do with the agency. It is incumbent upon the agency, then, to make the very best use of your time with the client.

"Wow, give me a shot at being a client."

When I was a client, I used a rule of thumb for agency attention. Under normal circumstances, I devoted about 10% of my time to the agency in direct contact, meetings, shoots, reviewing estimates, invoices, etc. If I needed to spend more than 10% of my time with them, to re-direct them, to review mistakes, to deal with agency personnel issues, then I was unhappy. If the agency could operate at a high level of productivity and take only 9% of my time, I was very happy.

A good account leader guards the client's precious time.

SHARED CLIENT OWNERSHIP

In the section "How to lose accounts," I stated that one key to survival for account leaders is to work on more than one account.

The corollary for the agency to survive is that more than one person must actively take ownership of each client member. The agency should never be totally dependent on one person to hold the account.

This lesson came to me in a very personal way. One of our largest accounts was run by an account leader who did a great job of winning over the client, becoming not only a business partner but friends and drinking buddies. So, on one level the account leader was doing a superb job of managing the client relationship. Except...

"THE LESSON STUCK WITH ME THAT AT LEAST TWO PEOPLE NEED TO BE RESPONSIBLE FOR EACH CLIENT MEMBER."

One of the agency partners started to hear about more work getting rejected than normal, more changes than usual, and a big increase in creative write-offs. The partner heard the account leader complain bitterly that the partner was interfering with "my account." Oops.

The partner asked me to work on the account, get to know the client, and discern whether or not the agency had a problem. The agency did have a problem — a big one. It turns out the account leader was recommending work that he personally favored, not the work favored by the creative group. He was trashing some of our work in front of this client. And, there were some questionable bidding arrangements made with a favored printer.

The story ended happily for the agency since ultimately both the account leader and the client were fired. But the lesson stuck with me that at least two people need to be responsible for each client member. You want to ensure continuity in case of turnover, and to maintain a set of checks and balances to keep relationships from getting too close.

CREATING INCREMENTAL REVENUE

In discussing the state of our business with agencies all over the country, I have learned two things: First, some agencies are growing at a very rapid rate, requiring a lot of new people. And secondly, many of these same agencies do not credit new business acquisition for much of that growth.

They are doing a great job of creating incremental revenue opportunities among their current clients.

Agency principals know that the very most profitable new business comes from their current clients. The cost of acquisition is little or nothing. The learning curve is very minimal, and in many cases fewer incremental employees need to be added compared to a whole new account.

"REMEMBER, IT IS MUCH EASIER FOR THE CLIENT TO HAND OVER NEW ASSIGNMENTS TO THE AGENCY THEY ALREADY KNOW."

Junior account leaders can make a great, and sometimes a greater, contribution than senior leaders to building revenue with an existing client. Juniors usually spend more time with their client counterparts than do the more senior managers. The opportunity to build trust can be tremendous at the junior levels. When new assignments surface, the junior managers may well hear about them first, and their client can often influence who gets the assignment.

Remember, it is much easier for the client to hand over new assignments to the agency they already know. Conducting a pitch costs clients the time, effort and lost productivity. A new agency requires time to learn the clients and their business with no guarantee that the work will be better. Clients dearly like to avoid breaking in new agencies.

So, how do you go about tapping into the golden bonanza of incremental revenue?

LISTEN. Your clients will talk about activities going on around the company, including areas where you might not currently have business. That discussion may come in the form of complaints about resources being diverted to another area due to a hiring freeze, or a pickup in sales, or an increased investment to create more business. Sales, Trade Relations, Public Relations, New Product Development, Market Research, Interactive, Promotion, Brand Identity, internal merchandising of new policies, are all potential gold mines for incremental revenue. Listen for the sound of unmet needs.

WANDER. When you meet at the client's office, make it your business to meet someone new or to catch up with someone

"UTILIZE BREAK-FASTS, LUNCHES, AND DINNERS TO GET TO KNOW PEOPLE."

with whom you don't frequently interact. This is so easy to do. Put another way, what would a competing agency pay to get access to the halls of your client just to get acquainted, enjoy a short conversation, inquire how business is going, etc.? Having worked on new business during my whole agency tenure, the answer is A LOT. So wander. We discussed "Multiple Agendas" in another section. Meeting people who might work on potential incremental revenue must go to the top of the Agenda-Additional Items list.

GET TO KNOW THEM. Utilize breakfasts, lunches, and dinners to get to know people. Get beyond their job functions (remember, clients wear three hats — job hat, corporate hat, and human being hat.) Follow up with a call, and stay in touch.

My boss of twelve years, Lloyd Jacobs, actually met me when I was working as a Brand Manager at a client company. He would say hello when we passed in the hall. One day he stopped into my office and we talked business for awhile. Then I picked up another brand, and who was my senior agency contact? Lloyd Jacobs. So when we created a new product line for that brand, guess who got the assignment? Yep, Lloyd and his agency.

Incremental opportunities with your current clients fly all around you. Learn how to listen, wander, and schmooze. Make sure you pick up more than your fair share.

INITIATE. Look for opportunities or make opportunities, to bring new thinking or ideas that the client may not yet know they need. For example, you might bring a PR person to one of your meetings in order to introduce a new face, a new asset for the client. Then maybe you present some PR ideas to your client. Maybe the client didn't know you possessed that core competency. Create business-building ideas, monthly. One great way to test the incremental waters of a client is to always present a media plan with an addendum: what could the client accomplish if they added (10%, 25%) to the budgeted plan? The dynamics inside a client company can change as quickly as they do at an agency. The incremental spend idea may not receive a lot of encouragement at the presentation, but if the situation shifts, you have created ideas that are ready to execute and the client knows you are ready.

Manage your senior people. Sometimes, you sense that an opportunity may exist, but you cannot make it happen at your level. Get the appropriate senior agency person to connect with their client counterpart to schedule a meeting, a dinner, and push for an assignment, or at least discern how real is the opportunity

WHEN THE AGENCY-CLIENT RELATIONSHIP ENDS

As noted in the section "Why Agencies Lose Accounts" you may have noticed that two of the three most frequent reasons have nothing to do with the agency's performance.

That is a reality of the business. It happens, it stinks, and no matter how or why an account is lost, you just feel plain bad. I am talking about an account you personally work on. When it's the other guy's account, you sympathize. When it's your account, its personal. You endure a horrible funk because you have worked so hard, sweated the details, pulled miracles out of the air, saved the client's behind on more than one occasion, and often felt like you and your colleagues really cared more about the client's business than did the client.

"OVER THE NEXT 90 DAYS THE AGENCY, LED BY THE ACCOUNT TEAM, CONTINUED TO OPERATE AT, AND EVEN ABOVE, THEIR NORMAL TERRIFIC LEVEL."

I pose this scenario of gloom and defeat for a very important reason. How you handle yourself and the account during the wind down period will speak volumes about you, your agency, and the integrity you live by.

I was told a story about an agency that lost a huge account due to a change in the senior marketing management position. It was a surprise, no a shock, for many reasons. Over the next 90 days the agency, led by the account team, continued to operate at, and even above, their normal terrific level. As it happened, the client ran into a crisis during the 90 day wind down period. The client was frantic. The agency people worked late nights to resolve the crisis. On a Saturday morning, the senior client walked into his conference room to meet with his team. In the conference room sat the account team from the agency. They all worked hard together and they solved the problem and averted the crisis.

A week later, the client called the president of the agency and told him how totally impressed he was that a terminated agency would rise to the occasion in this fashion. He then asked the agency president if they would consider continuing to handle the account. They said yes.

There are occasions when the agency decides they need to terminate a client. Admittedly, this doesn't happen with the frequency of the reverse scenario, but it does happen. There are a myriad of reasons why an agency may make this decision (profitability, demoralizing client, want to pitch a larger account in the same category, etc.) This decision is almost always made at the most senior levels of the agency. But the psychological effects on the account leaders may be very mixed. On the one hand, a problem client is removed from the roster. However, the account people have now lost an income stream that supports their salaries. This is a good time to take to heart the wisdom of working on more than one account if at all possible.

In this scenario, just as in the first one, how you handle the process will say a lot about you, your agency, and those values you say you believe in. You give at least 100%, make sure the service levels are at an all-time high, with zero mistakes, and you maintain your normal professional behavior right to the end.

Very often the account leader must communicate the bad news. Just recognize that this is an unpleasant task.

If at all possible, you should face your senior client in person. Put the resignation in writing. Be direct and to the point. "Pursuant to our contract, the X agency is terminating its relationship with the Y company, effectively immediately" is an example. Whether or not you provide reasons in writing or say them verbally is up to you. But keep the reasons on a high professional plane, e.g. "creative differences, change in direction, profitability…"

Assure the client that your agency will continue to provide service in the same manner as always for the duration of the phase-out period. Add that you would be happy to assist in any way possible to help them find another agency.

Make it clear that the turnover of materials and any briefings the client deems necessary in order to make a seamless transition will be handled in the highest professional manner.

Ensure that the team goes above and beyond to comply with the client's wishes in making the changeover.

However, the account team must also make sure that the agency is not taken advantage of during the wind-down, such as the client requesting the next year's creative being totally developed, etc. All new projects must include a discussion with agency senior management as well as the client in order that the expectations regarding new deliverables are extremely clear and in writing. An agency does not want to deal with a lawsuit brought by a scorned client.

Make absolutely certain that the agency is in no way financially vulnerable during the wind-down process. If your alarm bell in your head tells you to withhold work while you wait to get paid, listen to that bell.

In case you were wondering, you always feel much better when you are the terminator, not the terminee. Always.

~Notes~

~NOTES~

CREATIVE

UNDERSTANDING GOOD VS. GREAT CREATIVE

Relax. If a linear packaged goods marketer like myself can learn the difference, anybody can learn the difference.

Remember that developing taste in anything — art, music, ideas — is an acquired skill that requires viewing what experts think is great. Then practice, practice, practice making judgments until your confidence in that judgment increases.

Read the show books, just like your creative teammates do. When you look at award-winning work, ask yourself: Why did this work win an award? Then answer it. Repeat every month for a year. You will learn how great work evokes emotion, interest, and action.

When you are watching television, reading a magazine or newspaper, or surfing the internet, take 10 minutes every day and stop on ads and ask yourself: Do I like that ad, why or why not? It does not matter whether anyone would agree with your judgment or not. What matters is you are conditioning yourself to discern what you think is good, bad, and, rarely, great, ideas.

When you sit in a creative review meeting, ask your creative team:

"REMEMBER, IN THIS MEETING, IT IS NOT YOUR ROLE TO APPROVE THE WORK. SO, KEEP YOUR EVALUATIONS TO YOURSELF. BUT DO MAKE A JUDGMENT."

Why do you love this work? You then decide for yourself if you agree or disagree with them. Remember, in this meeting, it is not your role to approve the work. So, keep your evaluations to yourself. But do make a judgment.

Personally, I would not attend any seminar on creativity or listen to a lot of people tell you what is great, etc. If you get involved in seeing great work and wrestling with what makes it great, and then start judging work out there in the world, you will become an expert. Most people will not go to this trouble. I felt forced to do it because I was working at a world-class creative agency in McKinney and I didn't want to embarrass myself.

The point is, it worked for me. It will surely work for you.

GET CREATIVE!

David Baldwin, Executive Creative Director of McKinney, espouses the idea that everyone in the agency is creative.

Great ideas are not the sole purview, or the sole responsibility, of the "creative" team.

That being said, how do you go about getting creative? Do it the same way the creative teams do it; read the award books. Just kidding. The key is to get outside your routine. In other words, disrupt yourself. Disruption can occur either by yourself or with other people. Some examples:

BRAINSTORMING.
Not a new idea, but it can be very effective when done correctly.

"MOVIES THAT YOU WOULD NOT ORDINARILY WATCH AND MAGAZINES THAT YOU WOULD NOT ORDINARILY READ (MEN, READ SOME OF THE WOMEN'S MAGAZINES ONCE IN AWHILE) CAN GIVE YOU A POSITIVE CULTURAL JOLT."

Coaching tip: Ask to get sent to a seminar to learn how to a become a brainstorming moderator.

° The idea behind brainstorming is to get focused for a very short time and generate a lot of ideas.

° There are no bad ideas in brainstorming. You want to avoid putting your normal filters on ideas.

◦ This collaborative dynamic encourages everyone to get involved, not just the senior people.

◦ The short timeframe, no longer than an hour, also forces people to keep throwing out ideas.

◦ Judgments about ideas expressed should be immediately blunted. Extensive discussion about a particular idea should similarly be cut off.

The account leader should include people at any level who are outgoing, not afraid to express contrary opinions, and possess above average taste. In terms of numbers, I like to use more than three and less than ten people. With experience, you will develop your own sense for the right number.

GO OUTSIDE YOUR FIELD.
Advertising books are fine, you should read them all. But take a look at the reading list I included in this book. They are subjects that inspire me. Leaders like Margaret Thatcher inspire me. Mother Teresa lived the idea of service in a way that none of us will ever duplicate. The book, *Feel the Fear and Do It Anyway*, speaks to facing the anxiety that accompanies anything new, or foreign. It was not written for the ad business, but it sure does apply. The book, *Blink*, gives us a whole new perspective on processing thoughts. Inspiring.

Movies that you would not ordinarily watch and magazines that you would not ordinarily read (men, read some of the women's magazines once in awhile) can give you a positive cultural jolt.

DO SOMETHING NEW EACH DAY.
This is a simple way to disrupt yourself. Take a different route to work. Wear an outfit or combination you have never before worn. Or, on a more adventurous level, try something that totally disrupts your comfort zone. I took my teen-age daughter on an Outward Bound experience in the North Carolina mountains. We hiked up and down mountains with 50 pound packs on our backs. We slept on

the ground. We carried and prepared our own food. We rappelled down rock walls. We climbed up the rock faces (did I mention I was afraid of heights?) I didn't bathe for eight days. You get the idea. Major disruption. Major head-clearing. The world looked a whole lot different, more accessible, the possibilities more attainable after that major disruption.

ASK YOURSELF A RIDICULOUS QUESTION. THEN FIGURE OUT AN ANSWER. The question could relate to your private life or your work. For example, a life question could be "If I had six months to live, what experiences would I undertake?" "If I had one day to live, how would I spend it?"

On the work side, try this. "What would our client have to do to get 100% of the market?" Or, "Budget aside, what would I like to do to drive the business as high as possible?"

On this last question, a former Marketing Vice President made me go through just this exercise, but for real. He called it the "Billion dollar test market." I am not kidding. I took a very small market and translated a $1 billion marketing budget into this market. The questions were: can this brand be revived? If so, how high is up? What new marketing tools could we invent since money is absolutely no object. What an exercise. And talk about getting inspired about building a brand.

Try some of these creative juice builders. Don't let the creative team have all the fun.

LANGUAGE: YOUR MOST POWERFUL TOOL

One day an agency owner told me, "You are somehow able to push people aggressively without intimidating them or demoralizing them."

His comment stunned me. For many years, on both the client and agency side, a long-standing and justified criticism of me was that I corrected people in a way that left them feeling deflated. I was conscious of this fault and I had worked on improving my coaching technique for years. Apparently, I made some improvements along the way.

"WE LIVE AT THE CENTER OF THE ACTIVITIES IN THE AGENCY. WE COMMUNICATE WITH PEOPLE WHO POSSESS WIDELY VARYING LEVELS OF EXPERIENCE AND JOB EXPERTISE."

So I thought a lot about how I use language. How do we use language to become successful and what happens to cause us to come up short? This issue is so critical for account leaders to master since we live at the center of the activities in the agency. We communicate with people who possess widely varying levels of experience and job expertise.

The same goes for our clients. We deal with junior to senior clients, clients with work experience that can vary greatly and frequently is much different than our own.

I began to listen in meetings to how people used language and the visible effects it made on their audience. I also noticed that nearly all of us remain oblivious to those effects when we are speaking.

I want to share some suggestions that have enjoyed the most consistent success. I focused my personal research on creative people and clients, but the principles certainly apply to any functional team in an agency.

CREATIVES

Use questions. Negative declarations will cause creative people to shut down, stop listening or dig in. You will see the arms cross, the eyes wander or go glassy as they tune you out.

For example, if an account leader sees a concept that concerns them regarding whether it fits the strategy, two different approaches to raising the issue elicit very different responses.

Negative declaration: "That idea isn't even on strategy. The client will never consider it."

Question: "Bob, why do you love this idea, especially as it relates to the strategy of…?"

The point is that you get the issue on the table. In doing so, you do not create an us/them conflict which causes the digging in, the glassy eyes, etc. You always want to affirm with the creative team that you are there to help make the work as great as possible. You need your creative teammates to hear your concerns and consider them, not shut down.

Examples of other questions might be:

"What would you say to a client if they said…"

(When the creatives are behind schedule) "What do we need to do to get ready?"

Use solicitations. You are on the same team. The creatives don't work for you.

"Help me get around the client concern…"

"How do you think we should respond/handle that issue?"

"Give me your thoughts…"

Use positive declarations. Nothing says leadership like putting a stake in the ground. Your creative partners will respect you for it.

"I am going to sell this."

"That is a great idea."

"I get it. You've got something there."

CLIENTS

Clients are different from creatives (am I the master of the obvious or what?) Creatives need to know that you will fight for them and their work. Clients want and need to know that you are listening to them, and that you respect them.

So your language needs to speak to the clients' needs. For example:

Acknowledge:

"I see your point."

"We will do that."

"Let us think about it. We will get back to you (when)"

"Anything is possible."

"I can see you are troubled."

Ask questions:

> "What is it that you don't like?"

> "Can we have the freedom to come up with another solution?"

Clarify and Enroll (Invite participation and collaboration):

> "So, this is the problem we need to solve. Is that right?

> "This is what we will do next, given our discussion. Agree?

> "Let's close this discussion down until you and I can get on the same page. Ok?"

Keep the "corral" as wide as possible:

> "Please let us work on some other ideas in addition to your suggestion."

> "Let us get back to you with a better solution."

Please notice that nowhere in this language is the word "no." "No" is the ultimate negative declaration. It implies that not only can't the work or request get done, but that it won't get done. In addition, when account leaders use the word "no," they lose control of the meeting, the issue, and even the next action steps. You set yourself up for someone to say, "Ok, I will do it myself or I will find someone who can do it."

Practice listening to other people use language, and observe how language affects people. You will develop a sensitivity to your own language and its effects.

When you get a handle on how you use language, you will have added a powerful weapon to your account leader skill set.

SELLING THE WORK

"ACCOUNT PEOPLE CAN BE EVEN MORE CRITICAL TO SELLING GREAT WORK THAN CREATIVE PEOPLE."

I asked David Baldwin, Executive Creative Director at McKinney, to address a small agency I was running on the subject of great creative and building a creative culture.

On the subject of selling the work he shared these bits of wisdom:

° There are no good clients. That is a myth. What there are are smart people who need to solve a problem and they need ideas to do it. If the work is right, and you are solving their problem, then your job is to help them understand how it will help them. Only then will they buy it.

° Pre-presentation planning is critical to selling great work. Videos showing category sameness, putting ads in magazines to show the ad breaking through the clutter, etc. help create a proper environment for the client to understand and approve the work.

° Account people can be even more critical to selling great work than creative people. Good creative people can produce consistently good work The relationship between an account person and the client can make the difference in whether a client buys the work or not.

To David's excellent list I would add these points.

○ The best creative presenters should present the work. Makes sense, right? I cannot tell you how many arguments I engaged in with Creative Directors over whether the creative team that created the work should present it to the client. If the creatives are poor presenters of their work, someone else should present it. Presenting the work should not be a reward for creating the work. If creatives want to present their work, then they have to learn how to represent their work well.

It won't surprise anyone to learn that the batting average for good presenters is a whole lot higher than for poor presenters.

○ All account people must learn how to effectively present all forms of creative ideas. The approach to selling print is much different than selling radio, television, etc. The Creative Director or the best presenter of creative should conduct a "selling creative" seminar for all account people.

○ When preparing to present creative work, I liked to quiz the creatives regarding why they loved the work. Creative people process differently than we account people (you think?) and you can get clues for selling the work and language that will aid the sales effort, from listening to creatives talk about their work.

○ Sometimes, there is disagreement over what work should be presented, and which idea should be recommended. But once the decision is made, everybody who will be attending the meeting must get enthusiastically behind the decisions. Or stay home. The client will smell hesitation and internal agency conflict very quickly. If you cannot support the work with enthusiasm, do your team a favor and skip the meeting.

∘ Account leaders play a key role in a creative presentation even when the creative team is presenting the work. The creative person has the credibility of being the expert. But they are also assumed by the client to be self-serving. This makes it very difficult for creatives to defend the work. The account leader represents the objective marketing counsel who can help the client see that the recommendation represents the best of all options. See the section on "...Great Thinking" and learn how to analyze the pros and cons of each idea, and lead the client to the best one. Defending the work to the client in front of the creative team builds their confidence in the account team and strengthens the teamwork bond.

∘ Always begin a creative presentation by handing out and highlighting the creative brief. This discipline discourages clients from suddenly changing the brief on a whim. The agency immediately takes control of the meeting. A foundation is set from which the presenting team can roll into their set-up of the work.

∘ Learn how to set up each ad. It doesn't require a long lead-in, but each ad deserves to get its own presentation. The set-up should create a context that will prepare the client to understand, and approve, the idea. An example might be the following:

To set up a retail ad that uses a lot of white space instead of all copy versions like you usually see, you might say "We live at retail

"IF YOU CANNOT SUPPORT THE WORK WITH ENTHUSIASM, DO YOUR TEAM A FAVOR AND SKIP THE MEETING."

in newspapers in a cluttered, busy, screaming environment (show a sample retail section.) So to counter that environment, and to make our offer stand out, we decided to present our offer (then show the ad with the offer in the middle of the ad with a short headline, all of which is surrounded by white space.) In this case, you prepare the client to understand the advantage of using a very unusual ad design before they even see the ad.

When you are listening to a good presenter, notice how he or she sets up the ad so the ad itself gains momentum before the client sees or hears it.

◦ Practice. My recommendation is three times. After you go over your part three times, you should know it cold. Consult the pod on "Making More Powerful Presentations" to learn how to prepare and to deliver your presentation.

◦ Know when to close it down. As soon as you hear the approval words from the client, remove the work from sight. Do not give the client the opportunity to start second-guessing. Do not give a junior client the chance to throw a zinger into the discussion just to validate their presence in the meeting.

Similarly, if the meeting has not gone well, remove the work from sight, tell the client you and the team will re-group and get back to them in a timely fashion.

HANDLING CLIENT OBJECTIONS TO CREATIVE IDEAS

"MOST CLIENTS WANT THE AGENCY'S BEST THINKING AND RECOMMENDATIONS. THEY REALLY DO."

There are a few subjects that make account leaders absolutely cringe. Dealing with client objections during a creative meeting certainly goes on that list.

After all, they are the client. Their opinion obviously counts for a lot. It's their money…They have the final say…We don't want to get fired…Their idea is not that bad… There is not time to do it over so… The list of account-side generated excuses for not dealing with client objections goes on and on. I even heard this one from a very senior account person, "Its all subjective anyway, so who's to say the client isn't right?"

Well folks, having been a client for ten years, and having worked with clients for another 20+ years, let me give you a few tidbits of insight about most clients.

1. They really don't know what is the best communication for their business. Why? They have gone through precious little, if any, training regarding the craft of how to best communicate an idea. Nearly zero. The fact that they possess the title and have been issuing opinions on the subject for a long time does not necessarily mean they have

acquired the necessary expertise.

The backgrounds of some of my very senior clients have included plant management, law, finance, sales, purchasing and revenue forecasting, just to name a few.

2. Most clients want the agency's best thinking and recommendations. They really do.

3. Clients also want to know how to be a better client to the agency. No one ever taught them. Clients will allow an agency to show them, even lead them a little, regarding how to manage an agency for best results. If you do not believe me, show this section to one of your clients (so you are off the hook) and ask them if they think this makes sense. Send me a quarter if they agree!

I have listed several responses that I have used successfully over the years. Read them not so much for their literal meaning because you have no way of knowing the context of the remarks. Rather, read them as examples of an account person assuring the client that the agency wants what is best for the client's business. The agency requests the opportunity to find the best solution. The client should trust the agency to do just that. Also, clients want to see and hear conviction from their agency. It soothes their own anxiety and bolsters their confidence.

1. "With all due respect, your comfort on first viewing is not relevant. What's relevant is whether it is on strategy. The work is supposed to jar the comfort level, which means it doesn't look like everyone else in the category."

2. "Tell me everything you don't like about the ad. I want to understand clearly and completely. Then let our creative team develop the solution."

3. "Your (client's) solution might be the best one. But on the chance that our creative team can come up with a better solution, I would like you to give us the freedom to find one."

4. "Your changes have ruined/totally changed the concept. Let us go back and start over with this new direction."

5. "We will develop your requested changes. We would like the freedom to create concepts that we think will work better."

7. "I hear you. I think you won't like the outcome of your request because…We are open to try it."

8. "Let's stop right here. This is not the direction we agreed to. We need to stop work until you and I agree on the correct direction." (Take personal ownership for the direction of the creative, this is not the creative team's issue.)

9. "Telling me you will know it when you see it is not helpful. I can't do anything with that. Let's be sure we are clear on what we are trying to accomplish."

10. "Hmm, I wonder if I could offer an alternative suggestion/interpretation…"

11. "You told us you did not want to do work that looked like everybody else. But that is just exactly what those changes will look like."

12. "The big risk is not in doing something different. The big (financial) risk is doing something that looks like all the others because you will either get lost or people will think your advertising is for your competitor."

13. (When a client thinks an ad looks "too pretty to ring the cash register") "The discount in the promotion ad will work harder if the product has high perceived value."

14. "Let us look at it and think about it (client change) I will let you know how we think your idea will work."

15. When a client dictates a solution: "Let's step back. Help me understand what you are trying to accomplish. What will (client solution) accomplish for you? I request that we be allowed to find the very best way to handle your problem."

16. "We need your help in what to say. Our job is to tell you how to say it."

While I cannot guarantee these exact remarks will overcome a client's objections, I can tell you that these responses and similar remarks helped clients approve creative work that won virtually every award in advertising, and created huge marketplace success.

A Client Approves Great Work When A Client Feels Great Trust

"The client needs to take a leap of faith with the agency in order to jointly create great work."

Bob Doherty, former Chairman and CEO of McKinney, addressed an internal Account Service seminar many years ago. He reminded us that creating great work actually puts a greater burden on account people than if the work were not as great.

As Bob so eloquently explained it, great work by definition challenges our comfort level because it is new and unique. On the other hand, comfort derives from a sense of familiarity. Familiarity is the enemy of great creative.

The account leader's job is to help a client resist the temptation to judge the work based on a visceral sense of comfort. In fact, the best clients recognize this instinct and judge work based on its ability to move people, not create a feeling of familiarity. The client needs to take a leap of faith with the agency in order to jointly create great work. And that trust will not be created in the meeting. Trust is created over time when the agency does three things:

1. Keep your promises. If you promise the ad will be delivered on

Friday, keep your promise. If you cannot deliver the ad on Friday, several days before Friday you talk with the client and negotiate a new delivery date. Then that date becomes the promise you must keep. You also make an implicit promise to your client to create great work. When the work is not great, you may want to call the client and tell them the work is not good enough yet to show. Then you negotiate a new due date. As long as you don't make a habit of it, this candor almost always impresses the client.

By the way, when you develop the ethic of keeping your promises to each other within the agency, keeping those promises to the client will become much easier.

2. Value business results. I have lost count of the number of times it appeared that the account team cared more about the business results of our client than did the client! When you care about improving the client's results, you figure out how they keep score (sales, share, profits, same store sales growth, awareness, revenue per berth, etc.) Then you get the same periodic copies of those scorecard measures so you can look at the same data as the client. That way, you develop a sensitivity for the dynamics of their business and sometimes you can spot a problem before the client sees it. Then you can jump on the problem and create solutions.

One of our account leaders saw a slowdown in the advance bookings of one of the cruise products. We created several optional promotional ads that addressed different levels of severity of the eventual problem. When the client called and asked us to help fix the slow bookings on X ship, we asked them if we could present the ideas the next day! Which we did and boom, the ads were sold and the bookings increased.

3. Act as a true business partner. Sometimes we have to tell our partners things they do not want to hear. Sometimes we must take actions that are not in the agency's best short-term interest because it best serves the client's short-term interests. After analyzing the business situation facing one of our home furnishings accounts, we determined that the best course of action was to cut the advertising

budget for the second half of the year and use that money to either shore up profits or to give the salesmen some extra trade promotion money to boost inventory at retail. After making our presentation, and after assuring the client that the brand's equity would not be damaged by this hiatus, the client expressed absolute amazement. In fact, they quizzed us about how we could make up for our revenue shortfall. Our answer was, "We want to be your partners in the good times and the bad. We are going to be around a long time, as will you. Let's continue to work successfully together." Our working relationship lasted well over a decade to the mutual benefit of both of our companies.

While the entire agency contributes to a trust relationship with the client, an account leader is living that trust relationship every day. So, the more trust the account leader can build up for the agency, the more trust the client will grant to the agency.

"ACT AS A TRUE BUSINESS PARTNER. SOMETIMES WE HAVE TO TELL OUR PARTNERS THINGS THEY DO NOT WANT TO HEAR."

HOW TO WORK SUCCESSFULLY WITH CREATIVE PEOPLE

"FIGHT FOR THE WORK. I AM TALKING ABOUT BRINGING THE SINCERE ADVOCACY THAT COMES FROM KNOWING THAT THE WORK WILL SOLVE THE BUSINESS PROBLEM."

I showed up for work at McKinney after spending 10 years as a packaged goods marketing guy.

When I met the Creative Administrator, Charles McKinney's right hand person who ran the Finished Art Department, bought the art, and scared the crap out of account people on a daily basis, the first thing she said to me was, "You better understand that your job is to make the work the best it can be. Period."

How right she was. Over the years, I learned how to make my individual contributions to great creative work from my position as an account leader.

Do these things and your creative partners will definitely notice. Don't do these things and your creative partners will absolutely notice.

1. Build trust with the client before creative is ever presented. Lead the client to successful outcomes for his or her brand and for him or herself. Become a committed junior partner with your client. Keep your promises. Then ask the client to trust you when you show them work that makes them squirm.

2. Fight for the work. I am talking about bringing the sincere advocacy that comes from knowing that the work will solve the business problem. Both the client and the creative team can smell when that advocacy is sincere and when it is not. Everyone thrives on positive energy, especially your creative teammates.

3. Keep reinforcing the client's decision to approve the work well after the approval. Remember that the client will receive all kinds of unsolicited opinion and advice. Everyone from the CEO to the mailroom guy will unwittingly create doubt in the client's judgment, which can cause latent nitpicking ("I was thinking over the weekend about the work, and you know, the headline is sounding a bit negative…")

Help your client and your agency out by passing along positive comments from the sales force (whom you have made friends with, right? Now is the time they can really help you), other members of the client organization, the trade, or even company vendors. Creative folks tend to believe that once the work is approved, they can move on. Account leaders know that it isn't always so. Keep selling!

4. Resist downgrading the client in front of the creative team. Sometimes, of course, this is very difficult but clients get "favored client" status among creatives when there is respect for the client. Negative harping does not contribute positively to that feeling of respect.

Whether creative people will admit it or not, they depend on their account leaders to maintain a sense of stability and sanity, especially when instability and insanity appear to be taking over.

5. You are in charge of managing the creative process. From beginning to end and everything in between. You are accountable for the ultimate quality of the work. The creatives won't manage the process and they should not have to. They should stay focused on creating great ideas.

6. Give your creative teammates bad news in person. Don't hide behind a voice-mail or an e-mail. They appreciate the face to face

because it shows them respect as a valued member of the team.

7. Put your creative team on a pedestal in your client's eyes. Never, ever, badmouth them in front of the client. Merchandise your team as the Second Coming, capable of all things great and wonderful. As part of that process, you must be prepared to take the heat and blame sometimes in order to protect the aura of your creative team.

Creative people in our business are the super stars, the marquee act. Besides making creatives feel good, it is very good business for the agency when the client thinks that those huge fees are worth it because they have a top creative team working on their business.

~NOTES~

~NoteS~

PERSONAL GROWTH

ORAL PRESENTATIONS

No other medium of communication will have a greater effect on the perception of your ideas than oral presentations.

This goes for both clients and colleagues (especially bosses.) The reason for this is that you are presenting both your content and yourself when you make an oral presentation. A hidden truth of oral presentations is that their effectiveness relies so much on the perceived competence and commitment of the presenter to the ideas. Sadly, far too few account people ever learn the key to making powerful presentations and with it, the confidence that communicates that they are in control and in charge.

I call this key "The Circle." "The Circle" is a presentation technique that works opposite of the way most people learn to make presentations. It allows the presenter to focus his/her attention on the audience and establish a rapport with them instead of the material.

Most people prepare presentations by writing it out, then committing that content to memory or to a set of comprehensive notes. The thinking goes that you will forget

"PRACTICE YOUR ROUGH PRESENTATION OUT LOUD. YOU NOT ONLY WANT TO CHECK THE ORDER OF THE POINTS, BUT YOU ALSO NEED TO HEAR HOW THEY SOUND OUT LOUD."

the content unless you put it in front of you in some way. So most speakers either read their scripts or they focus so much on the written notes that they sound boring, unsure of themselves, and/or they lack real commitment and passion for the ideas they are presenting. In short, they commit to the content and make little commitment to the audience.

So, here is a very simple template for creating very powerful presentations. The template works exactly the same whether you are speaking to one person or a thousand people. It works the same whether the presentation is ten minutes long or two hours.

1. Make a written outline of your major points. There are no more than six major points in any powerful presentation.

2. Make sub-points under each major point. Note any audio or visual aids you may need.

3. Practice your rough presentation out loud. You not only want to check the order of the points, but you also need to hear how they sound out loud. It usually takes three practice runs to iron out the content, order and props.

4. At this stage, you have created the content of the presentation. It's fixed in your brain. You do not need a script. All you need to do is to create, and write down, on a single piece of paper (or note card) the transitions that move you from one major point to the next.

5. At the top of your circle, write down the first three or four words that you will use to introduce each point. "Before I offer..." might be an example. Those initial words will kick-start the content of the presentation.

Write down these transition words in a clock-wise direction on the paper. Again, use just enough words to kick-start the content. For example, the words "Our proposal..." is all you will need to write down. Why? Because you know what the proposal entails. If you need to add a couple of words underneath, like "Timing, Components, Benefits, etc." they can act as a reminder for you. Since you know the timing, the components, and the benefits, don't write them down, don't read them, don't memorize them. Talk with your audience. Make eye contact. Speak with commitment, passion, and authority. Move around if you wish. You are not locked or frozen by "the script." Oh, and if you say it in a different way or in a different order than you originally outlined it, who cares? No one but you knows that the order changed.

6. Write down the three or four words that you will use to start your exit from the presentation. For example, "This proposal..." or "Let me express..." are examples. Many speakers lose momentum at the end of their presentations because they have not created a definitive exit. These few words should kick-start your finish. Say it, then sit down.

7. Never say "thank you" to exit a presentation. It sounds weak. Finish your content, and stop.

I should insert a note here regarding PowerPoint. Don't use it. PowerPoint distracts the listener from engaging with you while they strain to read the slides. You lose the power that comes from eye contact, appropriate gestures, and the sincerity that your persona represents. PowerPoint almost always requires the lights to be turned down which is not a good environment for powerful selling.

My experience with people who learn this technique is that everyone improves their ability to make a presentation. On average, after only one or two attempts, the presenter gets the hang of it.

Simple and powerful.

YOUR JUDGEMENT OR YOUR CONFIDENCE IN YOUR JUDGEMENT?

I received great satisfaction from watching and helping young account people succeed, increase their self-confidence through those successes, and thereby grow as professionals.

One of the frustrations in watching that process was to watch young people hold themselves back from expressing an opinion, offering an insight, or taking decisive action when they were perfectly capable and competent to do so. I liked to remind them that, with 100% confidence, that their judgment about a subject was more sound that they thought. I guaranteed them that their confidence in their judgment would increase geometrically more than the quality of those judgments. I made this point to encourage account people to express their opinion, state their case, recommend an action. In many instances they would either be right or their view would give someone else a kernel to chew on that would lead to an important insight.

Smart young people are nearly always better than they (down deep) think they are.

"I LIKED TO REMIND THEM THAT, WITH 100% CONFIDENCE, THAT THEIR JUDGMENT ABOUT A SUBJECT WAS MORE SOUND THAT THEY THOUGHT."

COACH DEVELOPMENT

So I don't make my former Human Resources managers mad at me, let me say that I think that performance evaluations are valuable.

There are two problems with them, however. First, in reality they are performed once a year and they seldom if ever get referred to by the employee or the supervisor again. Second, performance evaluations tend to focus on what did not get done, which is not very motivating to your best performers.

> "IF I COULD STATE THE DEVELOPMENT ISSUE IN A SENTENCE THAT WAS USEFUL. IF I COULD USE A FEW WORDS, EVEN BETTER."

The most successful "improvement" conversations I have initiated focused on the employee's development. For example, "What should I be working on in order to grow?" The emphasis focused on the employee's future, not past. If done correctly, one central idea comprises the development discussion.

I wanted my employees to keep that single development idea in their heads all the time, not once a year. We would talk about it frequently and review progress. There was no time frame set for acquiring or perfecting this skill. We both decided when the employee had competently adopted the behavior.

Then we moved on to a new development issue. This is an on-going process, not a once a year obligation.

If I could state the development issue in a sentence that was useful. If I could use a few words, even better. If I could say it in one word, the employee had a good chance to focus on the issue and to really master that behavior.

Following are some of the development issues that I have used to coach individual employees:

DEVELOPMENT IDEA	COMMENT
"Thank you. I am sorry."	This employee needed to develop empathy and humility.
"Strategy."	This senior manager needed to sharpen her big-picture thinking.
"Options."	This linear thinker was an action dynamo.She needed to spend a little time upfront considering more than her first thought.
"Act" (verb)	This young account leader needed to trust herself more and just go for it.
"Poise"	This highly sensitive account leader needed to maintain his composure when the going got tough.

"I/We"

This senior manager needed to become more inclusive in his language to build a greater sense of team rapport. Use less "I" and more "We."

Employees respond very well to this coaching. When I observed the new idea in action, I made sure I acknowledged and congratulated them. This type of personal coaching communicates to employees that someone cares about their career and are willing to help them grow and succeed.

REPLACE YOURSELF

The business world is a very competitive place.

And advertising agencies are just as, if not more, competitive than any client company. So it's only natural for account people to want to protect or even hoard their hard-earned knowledge and experience.

While in some ways this instinct is understandable, I would like to propose a totally different approach that will serve you in a much bigger and more powerful way to help you accelerate your future career.

Adopt the personal mindset that your job is to replace yourself. Reinforce the idea with all of your subordinates, too. Most young account people don't realize that when they enable a junior to take some of the work off their desk, it in turn frees up the time to take work off of their boss' desk. And taking work off your boss' desk is what we usually refer to as "a promotion." More money, more subordinates and more responsibility naturally follow.

> "ADOPT THE PERSONAL MINDSET THAT YOUR JOB IS TO REPLACE YOURSELF. REINFORCE THE IDEA WITH ALL OF YOUR SUBORDINATES, TOO."

You're probably asking yourself, "If I replace myself, and there's nowhere to go, won't I be eliminating myself from a job?" Of course you will. That's the point. You don't want your job forever — just long enough to prepare you for the next job. If the agency is growing, chances are, there will always be room for you. But if the agency isn't growing, won't you be leaving soon anyway?

I tried to reinforce this "replace yourself" ethic as a Group Head. When your group buys in, you start to see people really helping each other succeed. The people in my group invariably got bigger raises and faster promotions than their counterparts.

Since my group was generating the most growth, profit, and creative awards in the agency, I received more than my share of rewards as well.

MENTORING: FIND ONE, BE ONE

Mentor |**men** · tôr|
A wise advisor, a loyal
friend, a trusted guide,
a teacher and a coach.

- Webster's Dictionary

A mentor represents a great deal
more than just your "boss."

Most employees want to grow and
progress in their careers. However,
most do not clearly understand
what they need in order to grow,
and they do not know how to go
about growing their careers. Since
there is so little formal training
or development done in agencies
today, most employees find that
they have to figure it out for themselves.

> "MOST EMPLOYEES WANT TO GROW AND PROGRESS IN THEIR CAREERS. HOWEVER, MOST DO NOT CLEARLY UNDERSTAND WHAT THEY NEED IN ORDER TO GROW."

We are not necessarily talking
about learning how to accomplish
tasks better (training) as much as
how to grow in the profession. For
example, young people may want to
discuss with someone how to ask
for a raise, what steps to take to
increase their skills, how to handle
a rude superior, sexual harassment,
proper dress, and a thousand other
questions.

I was blessed to be taught by
two mentors during my career.
Don Cushman was my college
debate coach and Communication

professor. He taught me how to think, how to analyze, and how to make an argument. As a mentor, he invented the concept of tough love. Cushman could make me feel like I was one of the smartest people in the country. He could also make me feel like the dumbest SOB ever.

My advertising agency mentor was Lloyd Jacobs. I have quoted him extensively in this book. Lloyd shared a lot of wisdom over the years. He protected me, and he helped me both personally and professionally in so many ways. He used an expression when he needed to give me some tough love. I wince at the words to this day. "Schofield, you aren't going to like what I have to say." Ouch.

My mentors held this thread in common: They would not let me be any less than my very best. They told me the truth. They held me to a high standard. They gave me a little more responsibility than I was ready for so I would have to stretch and work to succeed. I owe a huge debt to my mentors.

A mentor need not be a direct supervisor. A number of women who worked for me sought out, with my total blessing, a senior female whom they admired, to be their mentor. One young art director told me he thought of me as more of a mentor than his Creative Director. There are really no rules about who can mentor who, except one: Everyone in the agency should be able to name one person who they are mentoring and one person who is a mentor for them.

When you find someone you admire, simply ask them if they would be your mentor. Believe me, that person will be honored to be asked.

If you see someone whom you would like to offer assistance, just do it. Offer the young person encouragement and congratulations when they do something well. Make it easy for someone to become a mentee by being available to them in a complete way.

Either the mentor or the mentee can initiate a get together. The mentor should insure that periodic meetings are scheduled throughout the year. Obviously, everything discussed remains totally confidential. Lunch is a great time to hold mentor meetings.

While there doesn't need to be a formal agenda, it always helps if one or the other or both members of the mentor team bring some thoughts to share.

The life of a mentoring relationship lasts as long as it is mutually beneficial. When it ceases to be so, go find another mentor and someone else to mentor.

Mentoring can act like cement that strengthens the foundation of the agency. It was personally extremely rewarding for me. If you wonder what is in it for you to become a mentor, remember how you felt when one or two people in your professional or personal life showed a great deal of interest in you and helped you to grow in some way. After you absorb those memories, then simply pay it forward. You will make both our industry and your life better for the effort.

OWN YOUR MISTAKES

"ONCE A MISTAKE IS MADE, THE ONLY RELEVANT CONVERSATION IS HOW TO CORRECT IT."

No one likes to make them. And in this business, people don't tend to tolerate them — whether they are your clients or your colleagues.

Yet, we all make mistakes. And unless you just live under your desk, you have probably made a few.

Years ago, a client's CEO told me that he didn't believe anyone could be truly successful in business unless they had made some great mistakes. He was speaking, of course, in the context of trusting your instincts, taking occasional risks and following your own path to stand out from the pack. But he was also talking about the integrity of owning your mistakes when they inevitably occur.

By the way, the term "your mistakes" refers to your personal failings and the failings of those who report to you.

To own your mistakes you must have an aggressive attitude and be willing to take decisive action.

1. Acknowledge the problem as soon as it becomes evident. It's amazing how impressed both clients and colleagues can be when a mistake is quickly and openly recognized.

A very young account person came to me once, shortly after moving into my group. She thought she'd made a mistake and wanted someone to know about it right away. As it turned out, her predicament was actually a small issue that was easily corrected. But her integrity and self-confidence made a lasting impression on me. It should not come as a surprise that she was eventually promoted ahead of her peers — many of whom had more experience.

2. Don't play the blame game. Blame is a destructive waste of time that can make you appear both graceless and tactless. Once a mistake is made, the only relevant conversation is how to correct it. Correcting the system, process or person to avoid repeating the mistake can come later.

3. Act quickly to correct the problem. Time is your enemy. The longer it takes to correct a problem, the greater the loss — in dollars and in client trust.

UTILIZE YOUR HUGE ADVANTAGE

Having worked on both the client and agency side, I developed a mind-set that helped me operate successfully as an agency account leader.

I thought of my job as working with one hand tied behind my back in dealing with clients. After all, account leaders can't know as much about the client's business as the client. The client operates in an internal environment that affects their decisions that agency people cannot know as well as the client. In addition, the client always makes the final decision and account leaders never make the decision. The mental image of one hand tied behind my back made me work harder, prepare harder, and dig deeper to find solutions that the client could not find.

"THE MENTAL IMAGE OF ONE HAND TIED BEHIND MY BACK MADE ME WORK HARDER, PREPARE HARDER, AND DIG DEEPER TO FIND SOLUTIONS THAT THE CLIENT COULD NOT FIND."

There is, however, one huge advantage that account leaders possess over their client counterparts. That advantage is the enormous amount of seasoned experience in all phases of the communication process that is available to the account leader in the agency. The same cannot be said of the client. For example, a junior account leader may be reporting to a boss who possesses ten more years of experience. A junior client most likely reports to someone with two or three years more experience at most.

Since the account leader connects all the functions of the agency to the client, he or she can tap that broad, extensive experience every day. The agency is built that way. The client counterpart, however, faces silos of bureaucracy in order to get the same level of expertise to help them. From personal experience, silo bureaucracies is one major reason why it always seems that the client is attending a meeting and not making things happen.

"THAT ADVANTAGE IS THE ENORMOUS AMOUNT OF SEASONED EXPERIENCE IN ALL PHASES OF THE COMMU-NICATION PROCESS THAT IS AVAILABLE."

This book is intended to help account leaders make the best use of that huge advantage. Make sure you show your appreciation to all those experts who work with you in all the functions. Don't forget to tell them "thank you" when they save your behind yet one more time.

TIME
AND
MONEY

When you think about the resources at your disposal to make magic happen for your client, there are really only two: time and money (people resources go in the money category.)

Generally, though not always, the less time you are given to accomplish something, the more money you will need to accomplish it. I think this dictum passes the "makes sense" test, yet many clients either don't understand it or don't believe it.

And no wonder. How many times do we tell our clients a rush job costs more? Sadly, not often enough. In fact, agencies so often perform miracles on very little time and eat the extra costs of overtime, an extra creative team, etc. that the client comes to expect miracles for the same price. Said another way, the client suffers no consequences for demanding either short turn-around times, the same low price, or both.

"I CANNOT PROMISE YOU THAT ALL CLIENTS WILL ADHERE TO THESE TIMELINES FOREVER, BUT I GUARANTEE THAT THE SITUATION WILL IMPROVE."

While this situation has become increasingly more challenging over the last few years, the solution still sits in only one place in the agency — with the account leader.

Time

What can you do? The key here is to create time standards for getting different kinds of projects completed, discuss it with the client, explain how the timelines benefit them, get their agreement, and then deliver against that time promise without fail. Impossible, you say?

That is exactly what every account group at every agency told me. One very experienced account person told me point-blank, "You need to understand that we will lose our largest client when we give them these timelines. Period."

My response? "Well, that is always possible. I suppose the very worst things that could happen when you conduct this conversation are: someone shoots you, you get thrown out of the office, or they fire the agency. Now, I have been holding this conversation with clients for decades. None of those things have ever happened. The worst response I ever received, once, was "No." The most frequent response was "Oh, ok." I cannot promise you that all clients will adhere to these timelines forever, but I guarantee that the situation will improve.

I told this account leader, and the entire account group, that all I would insist on was that they conduct the conversation. We reviewed how to conduct it, particularly focusing on the benefits in quality ideas that the client would receive for the same, or lower, price.

In this case, all the account people went out, some very reluctantly, to talk to their clients about, ugh, timelines. The result was that every single client said some version of "Oh, ok."

The agency knows better than the client what is best for the client when it comes to time and money. When you show them what they need, and explain how it will benefit them, you have provided real leadership for your client.

A client once told me on a Friday that she wanted to see the concept on Tuesday. I asked when she needed it. "Oh, I have to present it to my boss on Friday." So I said, "that means that if we get an approved concept in your hands by end of day Thursday, you would have what you need?" She agreed. So I asked if we could have an extra day to work on the idea and give it to her on Wednesday. I explained that one day would permit our creative team to explore more than one option, to spend time working out which solution would be the most powerful, and I was confident that she would be pleased with the result. Again, she agreed. The creative team came through for her. Clients can be reasonable if you tell them what the agency needs from them in order to be successful. But you do have to show them the way.

Money

A solution to the money conundrum is to dare to show your client the "truth." That is, you show them an estimate to correspond with each production schedule. The "normal" schedule is attended by an estimate that is lower than the "hurry up" schedule. The client can choose. You do not have to tell the client "it can't be done." You say "it can and will be done. The cost to do it depends on how much time we are given."

By the way, the normal response by the client to this tactic is nearly always "what do I have to do in order to save that money?" Now, account leader, you have succeeded in getting the client on your side of the desk because they now understand the consequences of two different time/money options.

I promise, I have never lost either an account, or an account person, to gunshot wounds from showing the client how we could make the very best use of their time and money resources.

RUNNING A MEETING

We sit in more meetings than almost any other activity either in our work or private lives.

So you would think that we would all be experts at how to run a meeting, or certainly how not to run a meeting.

The basics are simple. The execution is not always so.

1. Start and end the meeting on time. Announce at the beginning of the meeting when it will end. If you are experiencing trouble in getting meetings to start on time, try setting the start time at an "odd" time, like 8:16 am. I can only report that it works like magic.

2. State the intended outcome of the meeting right after you announce when the meeting will end.

3. If the meeting will take more than 30 minutes, hand out a written agenda. If it will take 15 minutes or less, stand up.

4. The leader must keep the discussion on track. When people get long-winded, you need to close them off ("let's keep going" or "let's get back on track" or "we have beat this subject to death, let's move on.")

> "IF YOU ARE EXPERIENCING TROUBLE IN GETTING MEETINGS TO START ON TIME, TRY SETTING THE START TIME AT AN "ODD" TIME, LIKE 8:16 AM."

Remember, if you are running the meeting, it is your meeting, even if more senior people are attending. If they want to run a meeting, they can schedule one. "This is my meeting, guys" should do the trick.

5. The leader must exhibit a higher level of energy than the room.

6. The leader should summarize the action steps from the meeting at the end.

7. A great way to bring a meeting to an end is to stand up and say "Gotta go."

Then go.

THE MOST CRITICAL MEETINGS

I used to think that agencies held a lot fewer internal meetings than the client. Today I am not so sure.

As more and more individuals in the different functional areas take part in client meetings, there has occurred a coinciding increase in the number of meetings and the size of those meetings.

I want to offer a point of view on what I believe are the three most critical internal agency meetings for which the account leader is responsible. The success of these meetings will directly affect the success of the agency.

1. CREATIVE AND MEDIA BRIEF MEETINGS.

All agencies use their own forms to try to stimulate great thinking when it comes to creative and media briefs. The account leader can bring the meetings and briefs to life to create excitement for the project. Ultimately, the account leader needs to conclude these meetings by either knowing that the brief will generate great ideas or that the brief needs more work. The most successful briefing meetings I have participated in brought more con-

"THE SUCCESS OF THESE MEETINGS WILL DIRECTLY AFFECT THE SUCCESS OF THE AGENCY."

text to the idea than just words on a piece of paper. For example, a montage of the target, or a montage of competitive ads that all look the same might be ideas. We brought in cancer survivors to speak to the team at the briefing meeting about their experiences. That inspired us all.

The meeting should be limited to only those people who are creative enough to contribute to the brief. The reason is the brief should generate discussion, arguments, personal anecdotes about their connection to the product or service. The process of discussing the brief should in itself be thought of as part of the brief.

The meeting concludes when the account leader asks the senior most creative teammate, "Do you have the input necessary to create great ideas?" The answer is yes or no, not "its ok" or "it sucks but we will make something out of it." Whining is not acceptable. This document represents the foundation for making the agency work great. There should be no "settling" with briefs. Period. Great creative agencies don't settle. Great account leaders don't settle, even if it means they have to dig deeper.

2. MID-POINT REVIEW MEETINGS FOR CREATIVE AND MEDIA IDEAS

At some point between the briefing meeting and the presentation of the ideas, there is in most agencies a "let's see where we are" meeting. Charles McKinney always thought this meeting was critical to determining which of the initial ideas should be mined for the greatest potential. As such, the role of each person who attends the mid-point meeting must be very specific and defined.

- ◦ Creative — is responsible for explaining the ideas, both how the idea fits the strategy and what they love about the ideas. The creative team always makes the final decision regarding which ideas go forward. Share with the whole team any concerns you may be feeling about the ideas.

- ◦ Account — needs to ask are the ideas on strategy? What client objections should we prepare for and what are the answers?

Account people do not approve ideas or decide what ideas go forward. Account people can offer input to improve the ideas. In this meeting, it is critical how the account leader uses language to insure the best thinking emerges from the meeting. "What do you think about…" creates a lot more esprit than "No way the client is going for that…" Limit the declarative sentences, maximize the use of the question.

○ Production (if permitted) — Your role is to assess any logistical or cost challenges that the team should consider as they take the ideas forward. Your opinions about the ideas should be kept to yourself unless invited by the creative team.

○ Traffic/Project Management — Your role is to get familiar with the ideas so you can manage the project through to presentation. Your role is not to offer opinions unless invited by the creative team.

The reason there should be a limited number of people who provide input in this meeting is that there is a very delicate process transpiring between the creative and account team members. The creatives are trying to figure out where some of the ideas are going, which ones have more power, and how to get the client to approve them. The creative team needs to dialogue with the account people in order to obtain the most insightful possible input.

3. PRE-PRESENTATION MEETING

In the inevitable rush to finish work that will be presented to the client, too many times this critical step is ignored. Yet the work deserves to get the very best presentation to the client. The client deserves to get the very best presentation of the work so they can understand why the recommended ideas will succeed.

The pre-presentation meeting should review the agenda that the account leader has prepared. Every piece of work that will be presented should be shown in its final form. Each speaker should rehearse their comments so that all attendees feel comfortable in the meeting with what is coming next. All props and set-up devices (charts, pictures, videos, music, etc.) should be present to insure everything works. All travel logistics, times, and the material check-list should be reviewed one more time.

This meeting can be very short. The key is for all attending agency members to feel confident and comfortable when they walk into the room and share some great ideas that will move the client's business.

MULTIPLE AGENDAS

One day, I was telling our Media Director about how we account people always create multiple agendas when we plan a client meeting.

She was curious to learn more, though I think she really thought I was full of b.s.

I told her, "When an account manager visits a client for a meeting, they possess an invaluable opportunity to accomplish so many more things than just the stated purpose of the meeting. So I always prepare several additional agenda items that I want to cover.

Examples:

° Meet someone you have not met before. Just tell them who you are and that you wanted to make their acquaintance. It may be the CFO, the head of Purchasing, R&D, whatever.

° Touch base with someone with whom you have not talked recently. It may be the CEO's assistant, a junior client, etc. Remember, those junior clients grow up to be senior clients. They will appreciate the attention.

> "I ALWAYS PREPARE SEVERAL ADDITIONAL AGENDA ITEMS THAT I WANT TO COVER."

○ Lay seeds for a future meeting or an idea, e.g. "We are starting to think about your trade problem. We will be scheduling something soon to give you our analysis and recommendations."

○ Schedule a breakfast, lunch, or dinner (everybody has to eat!) with someone to discuss an idea, get to know better, etc. Meals are great avenues for getting clients to relax their corporate guard. Plus, meals don't take away from the client's work day.

○ Drop off an article, an ad, some competitive tidbit in person.

○ Introduce someone, like your boss or the art director, to someone they have not met before, especially junior people.

When I hear a client say "we should get you guys an office since you are here so much," I know the team is accomplishing so much more on our client visits than just merely the stated agenda.

COLLATERAL IS A VALUABLE RETENTION DEVICE

Some agencies love to produce collateral for their clients. Some agencies hate it and don't do it.

I think those agencies that shun collateral work deprive the account leader, and thereby the whole agency, of a great opportunity to build and cement relationships with the client.

First, producing collateral almost always involves other departments in addition to Marketing. Sales, Customer Service, the dealers, Product Development, even Research and Development. So the agency gets to know and become known to these other groups and generates a good "buzz" inside the company, which of course the client hears. Obviously, good feedback about the agency from R&D elevates the stature of the client and their good judgment in hiring such a fine firm.

"THE AGENCY GETS TO KNOW AND BECOME KNOWN TO THESE OTHER GROUPS AND GENERATES A GOOD "BUZZ" INSIDE THE COMPANY, WHICH OF COURSE THE CLIENT HEARS."

Our agency prepared a whole year's worth of advertising and collateral for one client, which we presented to their national sales meeting. We produced a big dog and pony show. We showed everything from television ripomatics, beautiful print ads, and lots of collateral. The agency received a standing ovation for…postcards that travel agents could mail to their customers. Amazing. The sales force became a huge fan of the agency inside the company.

Second, collateral assignments give the agency many more opportunities to meet with and be seen by client employees. This presence breeds a very positive familiarity. One day, while walking the halls of my client, I was stopped by an employee in Customer Service. She asked me if I had created those new brochures. She said, "thank you for reminding me why I am proud to work for this company."

Internally, collateral pieces can help create enthusiasm for your account and retention among young creative people when they get a chance to flex their creative muscles on a project that is their very own. Many of McKinney's future stars created some of the most outstanding collateral pieces. They worked days, nights, and week-ends. They flagged me down when I was walking through the finished art department to pepper me with questions, to show me what they were working on. Their enthusiasm got me fired up. And the brilliance of the work reflected that enthusiasm.

So, collateral is an account leader's friend. And the margins make a nice contribution to those year-end bonuses as well.

HOW TO GET PROMOTED

Over a 30 year career, I wish I had a dollar for every time a subordinate asked me, "How long will it take for me to get promoted?"

My answer to that question was always the same. "I have no idea. It is not up to me. You will tell me when you are ready to be promoted." Of course, I had to explain that I did not literally mean they would tell me. By their actions, it would be obvious to me and people around them that they were ready for more responsibility.

So, what did I see that told me when someone was ready for promotion? Really, its quite simple.

"WANT TO KNOW ONE OF THE SUREST WAYS NOT TO GET PROMOTED? DO JUST WHAT YOU ARE TOLD."

I suspected a junior account leader was ready for promotion when he or she brought ideas to the table that no one else thought of, and no one asked for. And they made sense.

I suspected a mid-level account leader was ready for promotion when he or she disagreed with me, pointed out why I was wrong, told me about three better options, then told me the pros and cons of those options, then told me the best option.

I suspected a senior level account leader was ready for promotion when I went home knowing that if I did not come in anymore, everything would be just fine.

Want to know one of the surest ways not to get promoted? Do just what you are told.

TERMINATING AN EMPLOYEE

The Golden Rule helps a lot here: Do unto others as you would have done unto you.

Of course, you must have created documentation regarding poor work performance and a trail of conversations with the employee to both inform them of their shortcomings and action steps to improve their performance.

But the moment may come when you know in your head that the agency's best interests will be served by terminating an employee. Here are some guidelines to help you successfully navigate this unpleasant task.

First, the emotional side must be considered. You are taking away a person's livelihood. And be aware that the emotional side does not get easier with repetition. It always hurts to fire someone. It is supposed to hurt. If it ever ceases to hurt, you should find something else to do, preferably something that does not involve people.

Now, as for the process side, I have found that these suggestions offer the most humane approach for the terminee and yourself. They also protect the agency.

"BE AWARE THAT THE EMOTIONAL SIDE DOES NOT GET EASIER WITH REPETITION. IT ALWAYS HURTS TO FIRE SOMEONE."

1. Tell them in person.

2. Bring someone into the room to act simply as a witness. They should say nothing and they should make no reaction to anything that happens.

3. I recommend that the witness be the same gender as the terminee. It goes without saying that the witness should be someone that you trust to handle the situation in a mature fashion.

4. Be direct, brief, and clear. "John, I am going to terminate you, effective today." If this approach sounds harsh, consider how agonizing it would be for the employee to hear a speech when they will have a very good idea what is coming before you finish.

5. No reason needs to be given.

6. Keep it short. Provide details of the separation agreement, including logistics about vacating the office, turning in keys, picking up their personal stuff (I recommend that a time be arranged to meet the employee at the office when the office is closed, like the week-end.) Obviously, the employee will be in shock so you need to speak slowly and be as clear as possible. Invite the employee to contact you if anything is not clear once they have left the office.

7. Do not react to anything the employee may say. If there are tears, hand them Kleenex. If they ask you why, do not provide reasons. "It was a decision that I made in the best interests of all concerned" is about all that should be said. You need to understand that anything said in that meeting may come back in a lawsuit against the agency. That is also why you want to include a witness to verify everything you say.

8. I recommend that the employee be asked to leave the building immediately. Obviously, all situations are a little bit different. But most of the time, the employee will want to leave. Also, there is always a possibility that an immature person could spread a great deal of vitriol throughout the agency in a very short time.

9. Wish them good luck. Then someone in authority should escort them to their office, then to the door or elevator.

This is definitely one of the least tasteful situations you will ever face in your career.

MANAGE YOUR CAREER

In the same way that account leaders receive woefully little training regarding how to do their job, career management is also largely left up to each of us. That is not a bad thing.

It does mean that you need to take stock every once in a while to make certain that you keep yourself on track, or change your track in order to create a successful and satisfying career.

Here are some thought provokers that come from my own experience in proactively managing a career over many years.

1. Make career moves that will increase your Income Potential(IP). I hear young account people say they want to change jobs to get closer to home. That is fine, but that criteria will not, by itself, increase your income potential at all. In fact, it can reduce your IP in many cases.

One great way to increase your IP is to study the senior managers in your agency. Ask yourself, "what do they know how to do that I need to learn so I can make what they make?" I asked myself that question when I

"THE RULE I LEARNED TO FOLLOW WAS WHEN MY LEARNING CURVE FLATTENED, I LEFT."

was a young Brand Manager. I decided that the biggest difference in my skill set and the VP of Marketing was "strategy." He always came at issues from a strategic point of view. Whether the issue was corporate, financial, product, or marketing related, he always brought a strategic focus.

So, I devoted myself to becoming a strong strategic thinker. That skill definitely increased geometrically my income potential. Eventually, I turned that potential into reality.

2. Let your learning curve guide your career moves. If you are reasonably intelligent and reasonably ambitious, your sense about whether your learning curve is increasing, flattening or decreasing will serve as a great guide.

The rule I learned to follow was when my learning curve flattened, I left. As long as I felt (and you know this in your heart) that my learning curve was increasing, I was increasing my income potential. If I was learning at a high level, I was growing and producing. Coincidentally, raises and promotions always followed.

Do not succumb to the typical reasons people mention for making a job change:

○ I am frustrated
○ I am overworked
○ I don't like my boss
○ I am disappointed in my last raise or bonus
○ Other people got promoted ahead of me
○ I am tired of working on this account

These are short-term nuisances that can change and therefore are not smart reasons to uproot your career. Every time you change agencies, at any level, you must prove yourself all over again to a bunch of strangers

An executive recruiter whom I greatly admire once told me, "The time to leave is when you conclude that you cannot achieve your career goals at your current company." That is another way to put it. I like thinking about learning curves because you cannot fool yourself.

3. You must get better every year or you become obsolete. This applies to the most junior and to the most senior account leader. Our business is harsh that way. The expression "what have you done for me lately?" might have been created by someone in our business.

4. Figure out who are the really smart people around you, no matter their function, level in the organization or amount of experience. Listen well and take good notes when those smart people are talking. And, dismiss or ignore advice you get from people whose talent you do not respect. Sure, dumb people can come up with something useful once in awhile. But, if you have to bet, bet on the smart one. By the way, pick one of those really smart ones to be your mentor.

~NOTES~

~NoteS~

THE KEY TO ENJOYING A BALANCED LIFE

When I was getting started in the agency business in the mid 1980's, there were very few married employees and only a handful of children among 70 employees in the agency.

For many people, their agency work was their life. Many of these people were extremely competent, very focused and highly successful at work.

I had decided several years before I joined my first agency that I wanted to "have it all — " a successful career and a wonderful home life. I was very determined to do whatever it took to accomplish both. This sentiment was no more popular in the 80's than it is today. But I did it. I am so thankful that I did do it. And, if I can do it, anybody can do it.

Let me share with you how I did it.

First, I adopted the attitude that I would do whatever it took to grow and get promoted in my job. That meant that I did not "do all I could" until 5:30. It meant that I worked until 7:00p.m., 8:00p.m. or later

> "I HAD DECIDED SEVERAL YEARS BEFORE I JOINED MY FIRST AGENCY THAT I WANTED TO "HAVE IT ALL — " A SUCCESSFUL CAREER AND A WONDERFUL HOME LIFE."

sometimes. But since I am not much of a night person, I run out of gas after about 7:00p.m. So I came into the office much earlier than other people, say 6:30 or 7am. It was quiet so I could get a tremendous amount of work done before the phones started ringing and the meetings started. Also, before children, I liked to go into work in the morning on Saturday and Sunday for a few hours to either catch up or to think in a quiet environment.

I also observed how more senior managers managed their work. I figured that they had more to worry about than I did so they must have figured out how to get their work done in a more efficient manner than me.

Once our child was born, I stopped going into the office on Saturday and Sunday unless it was something important. Instead, I got up earlier in the morning to read or work at home before I went to the office.

As I became a manager, I worked very hard to teach and coach my subordinates so they could stand in for me if I needed to attend one of my daughter's events. Also, I boldly manipulated client meetings in order to allow me to attend family events.

What I learned was many meetings are scheduled in a fairly arbitrary manner. That was proved by how relatively easy it was for me to get clients to change the date or the time of meetings. Once I figured that out, my ability to "have it all" was not that hard to accomplish.

A female employee came to me once and said, almost defiantly, "No matter what you say, I am going to start leaving the office at 5:30 on Tuesdays so I can have dinner with my son." I smiled and told her, "First of all, why don't you leave each evening at 5:30 so you can have dinner with your son? Figure out how your work can get covered (lean on subordinates, re-schedule meetings, etc.) and commit to it. The only person who is keeping you from keeping this schedule is you. In fact, I bet you can't get out of here one day out of the week by 5:30 because you won't commit to it."

Sure enough, the very next Tuesday, I wandered by her office at 5:50. She was there. I just smiled at her at pointed to my watch. She said "I am leaving in five minutes." I just reminded her as I walked away, "its all up to you."

My old boss, Lloyd Jacobs, used to tell me, "Look, you control your own work hours. If you are not busy on some days, get out of here. Play with your daughter, run some errands, whatever. When the call comes for everyone to jump into the lifeboat, however, I don't want to hear anything other than 'give me an oar.'

Folks, you will not succeed in this business if you adopt a "9-5:30 attitude." As far as I am concerned, there is no excuse for not enjoying a fulfilling, successful career, as well as a wonderful family life. If I can do it, you can do it.

COACHING TIPS

Over the years, I have learned so much from so many bright people. Mostly, I learned what to do.

Sometimes, I learned what not to do. Either way, I share these miscellaneous tips with you in the hope that you accelerate your learning curve with some of these hard-learned do's and don'ts.

"SOMETIMES, I LEARNED WHAT NOT TO DO."

○ Write down every promise you make to someone. Write down every promise someone makes to you. Put those promises in time.

○ Tell people bad news face to face. Tell people good news any way you want.

○ Junior clients grow up to be senior clients. Be nice.

○ Clients can move to other companies. Be nice.

○ You can only learn something when your mouth is closed.

○ Don't talk over people. They can't hear you.

○ Never meet with your boss to discuss a problem without providing at least one solution.

- There is a solution to every problem.

- There is nearly always more than one solution to any problem.

- Agencies own the accounts. Account people just work on them.

- When your subordinate makes a mistake, it is your fault.

- Never tolerate abuse of yourself or your subordinates from either colleagues or clients.

- If you must use PowerPoint, you are most likely not prepared.

- When you say it, keep it short. When you write it, keep it shorter.

- If you must read your presentation, pass it out. It's less boring that way.

- People buy your content after they buy you, not the other way around.

- If you don't write it down, you won't do it.

- When you hold up a meeting of ten people for ten minutes, you have cost the agency 100 minutes. If you do it once a week, you waste over two months of one person's time.

- It is a sin to be unprepared. It is never a sin to be over-prepared.

- If you don't understand what I tell you, then it is I who am unclear.

- Sometimes, providing account service makes us lose our patience. Always, providing account servitude makes us lose our soul.

- If it takes an account leader ten contributions to create trust with creatives, it takes one betrayal to lose it.

° When you admit a mistake, it takes ten units of effort to correct. When you fail to admit a mistake, it takes 1000 units of effort to correct it.

° When you can't create the time to do it right, you can always create the time to do it over.

° The best clients understand that they always pay. They pay in money for giving poor direction. They pay in quality when they demand it overnight.

° The best clients understand that agencies must make money.

° The best clients know that the way to squeeze the most out of an agency is to pay them fairly, make the agency want to kill for them, then ask for the moon.

° If you don't look into the eyes of your creative colleagues, you don't really know if they "get" the brief. Same for media.

° Great work comes from rubbing intellects together in constructive conflict.

° Two people can defeat an army with an idea.

° Account leaders get the quality of creative thinking that they deserve.

° Clients think agencies do not understand or care about business. Agency people think they could run the client's business better than the client. Both are wrong.

° An account leader creates very little real contribution sitting in his office.

° Immediately after a client meeting, de-brief about what went right. The next day, de-brief about what went wrong.

◦ When you criticize a colleague, always use positives as well as negatives. The positives must be as specific as the negatives.

◦ Mature account leaders know that it is less important what I do than it is what I get done.

◦ We work in a business that does not tolerate mistakes. We all make them.

◦ If a meeting does not result in action, then people were just eating lunch.

◦ When you know you are right and they are not listening, pound your fist. You will be heard.

◦ Today's excellence becomes tomorrow's standard.

◦ Our business does not discriminate based on youth. It does discriminate, brutally, based on talent.

◦ Clients hire and pay for potential. Agencies hire and pay for performance.

◦ Great creative work does not come out of the end of a machine after you put a brief into one end. You must live with the project and the creative team at every step of the process. The creative team needs you, even if they don't admit it.

◦ Learn to give your boss a "30 second account update." This is a great discipline for you to sift away all the stuff going on and to synthesize the key issues of the moment. Thinking this way forces you to put yourself in your boss' shoes and figure out what he would want to know.

This discipline gives your boss a high degree of confidence that you are on top of the business. Hint: bosses want to know what is going wrong, off track, doesn't meet our expectations, the negative stuff. And your boss wants to know what you are doing to fix the problems.

○ There are only two relevant questions to ask when the agency has made a huge mistake:

How do we fix it?
How do we make sure this never happens again?

○ You know you have created the ideal creative or media brief when your colleagues read it and say: "We have no questions."

○ At the conclusion of one of your account group, status or production meetings, ask everyone to take out a paper and pencil. Pick a person and ask the rest of the group to write down what they appreciate about the chosen person. No talking, just fold up the paper and give it to the person, then go about your day. You just made theirs.

○ Its ok to feel uncomfortable. Your body is speaking to you. If that discomfort is uncertainty, figure out how to reduce it. If the discomfort is due to adrenaline, your body is sharpening your senses to win. If that discomfort is guilt, then clear it up with the person who caused the guilt. The only mistakes you can make when you feel uncomfortable are to not listen and to not act.

○ Sometimes an idea stinks. No doubt about it. No excuses, no rationalizations, no "the client didn't give me enough time/direction/money..." If you think it stinks, you are probably right. Acknowledge the truth. It can free you to do something great.

○ You are not a leader because you possess a title. You are a leader when someone is willing to follow you.

○ Acknowledge someone when they go above and beyond. A note is great. A face to face is even better. Saying it in front of other people is invaluable. Think how you felt when it happened to you.

○ The words "Thank you" and "I apologize" can never be stated too often. They get the greatest return on investment. The residual effects last longer than a raise.

○ The stories people tell about the agency make the agency unique. Without the stories, the agency is just another place to work and to earn a paycheck.

○ When the client is overworked or short-staffed, volunteer an account person to work at the client's office. The gratitude expressed by the client will exceed that of the biggest creative award they ever won.

○ Experience is sometimes overrated. Success speaks for itself.

○ Clients don't give away their products and services. Why do we?

○ Doctors, lawyers, and architects charge for their expertise. Why don't we?

○ Teach a client how to be a good one. If you use the right language (see section on Language) they will listen. Clients don't want to be bad clients. No one ever taught them the difference.

○ Much of successful account leadership is taking a "swing at the plate." I tell young account people I can teach them how to hit. I can guarantee that the ball will not hit them. I even assure them that if they swing that they will hit the ball somewhere. But only they can take the bat off their shoulder and swing.

○ Junior account leaders don't always realize that senior people are watching. Senior account leaders don't always realize that junior people are watching.

○ All account leaders get knocked down. No exceptions. The good ones know how to get back up and keep performing. And they don't get knocked down twice for the same misdeed.

° An account leader adds value to the client's business and to the agency's equity when he or she tells a client something the client didn't know.

° Your boss is not obligated to get along with you. It's the other way around.

INSPIRATIONAL READING LIST

The books on this list represent uncommon examples of leadership and innovative thinking.

Some books get read, then forgotten. I recommend these books because I gained some valuable insights that I use in my everyday work. I hope they do the same for you.

A Mind At a Time
- Levine

A Simple Path
- Mother Teresa

Bang
- Kaplan Thaler

Blink
- Gladwell

Communication and High Speed Management
- Cushman, King

Communication Best Practices at Dell, GE, Microsoft and Monsanto
- Cushman, King

Creative Company — St. Jude
- Law

Discover Your Genius
- Gelb

The Downing Street Years
- Thatcher

Emotional Intelligence
- Goleman

Feel the Fear and Do It Anyway
- Jeffers

The Female Advantage
- Helgesen

First, Break all the Rules
- Buckingham, Coffman

Freakonomics
- Levitt, Dubner

Good to Great
- Collins

Killer App
- Downes, Mui

Primal Leadership
- Goleman, Boyatzis, McKee

"I GAINED VALU-
ABLE INSIGHTS
THAT I USE IN MY
EVERYDAY WORK."

SUMMARY

A senior account leader recently told me that the major strength of his department was the great relationships they had forged with their clients.

In fact, he said that his clients had become "kind of friends." He admitted that their relationship made it hard for him and his team to "push back" in advocating new ideas that the client might not approve or defending ideas in the face of objections.

I asked this account leader if he thought the agency would be in a stronger position with the client under which of the following two conditions: if he managed his clients to make them happy or if he managed his clients to make them successful.

He didn't say a word. He knew the answer. After reading this book, I hope you do too.

Mark Schofield

~NoteS~

~Notes~

Printed in the United States
108103LV00004B/442/A